PENGUIN BOOKS

Extra Confessions of a Working Girl

D0465761

ABOUT THE AUTHOR

Miss S is a highly successful London-based paid companion. She began her career as a part-time working girl in a brothel whilst she was a student, before moving on to agency work as an escort. She is now fully independent. Miss S is intelligent, articulate, hard-working and ambitious. Above all, she loves what she does.

Extra Confessions of a Working Girl

MISS S

PENGUIN BOOKS

PENGUIN BOOKS

Published by the Penguin Group
Penguin Books Ltd, 80 Strand, London WC2R ORL, England
Penguin Group (USA) Inc., 375 Hudson Street, New York, New York 10014, USA
Penguin Group (Canada), 90 Eglinton Avenue East, Suite 700, Toronto, Ontario, Canada M4P 2Y3
(a division of Pearson Penguin Canada Inc.)
Penguin Ireland, 25 St Stephen's Green, Dublin 2, Ireland (a division of Penguin Books Ltd)
Penguin Group (Australia), 250 Camberwell Road, Camberwell, Victoria 3124, Australia
(a division of Pearson Australia Group Pty Ltd)
Penguin Books India Pvt Ltd, 11 Community Centre, Panchsheel Park, New Delhi – 110 017, India
Penguin Group (NZ), 67 Apollo Drive, Rosedale, Auckland 0632, New Zealand
(a division of Pearson New Zealand Ltd)
Penguin Books (South Africa) (Pty) Ltd, Block D, Rosebank Office Park,
181 Jan Smuts Avenue, Parktown North, Gauteng 2193, South Africa

Penguin Books Ltd, Registered Offices: 80 Strand, London WC2R ORL, England

www.penguin.com

First published in Penguin Books 2008
This edition published 2012
001

Typeset by Rowland Phototypesetting Ltd, Bury St Edmunds, Suffolk
Printed in England by Clays Ltd, St Ives plc

ISBN: 978-1-405-91163-4

www.greenpenguin.co.uk

Penguin Books is committed to a sustainable
future for our business, our readers and our planet.
This book is made from Forest Stewardship
Council™ certified paper.

ALWAYS LEARNING   **PEARSON**

Contents

1. *Fancy a Dance?*

It was my first real shift after my trial nights at the stripclub a few weeks back, and I was a bag of nerves. I shouldn't have been but I was. This time I didn't have friends close at hand to give me support if I needed it. My first night would be a slow one, I had been told, and I had spent most of it standing in the corner watching, so no wonder I hadn't made much money. But I was determined to give this dancing thing a good try. How hard could it be? Everyone kept saying it had to be better than selling your body, though I couldn't say I really got the distinction. And this was London: surely it had to pay better than working in a brothel in a provincial town?

The keen girls, primped and preened in their tight, sparkly dresses, arrived early. They dashed here and there, smelling of hairspray and stale smoke, trying to look their best so as to catch the attention of any man who came in. Everyone was on a real mission to make money, and it didn't stop at the girls who were dancing. You'd catch a glimpse of the odd waitress liberally applying lipgloss in a passing mirror in the hope of getting even the smallest tip to supplement her low wages.

The girls at the stripclub (sorry, 'gentlemen's club') seemed to be split between the girls who did and the girls who didn't – that is, the ones who would go off with clients at the end of the night for a better tip, and the rather snotty ones who proclaimed that they were 'dancers' and 'artists' and would never stoop that low, bla bla bla. I had gleaned that much from the natter that had gone on in the poky dressing room while the girls were getting ready.

That was the first of many revelations that night. More were to come from a fluffy, sour-faced blonde I soon had tagged as Miss Priss.

I was standing at the side of the main stage in the club. It ran along the back wall of the dark room, with rows of seats and small tables spread before it.

'Hi, you're new here, aren't you, love?' The sour-faced blonde leaned over in my direction.

I looked away from the stage and my view of the girl performing on it. She had big boobs and was shaking them in the face of some poor chap in the front row. He was there by himself, blushing, hands in his lap covering what looked like a prominent bulge.

As it was the start of the night there weren't many girls or guys around. By the look of the near-empty club, not all the girls were in by a long shot, and there was me already dressed and ready for action – if you could call it dressed. I was nervous as hell, as all the girls I had tried to spark up some kind of rapport with in the dingy closet dressing room had just shrugged and pointed when I'd asked them anything, or totally snubbed me. One just grunted at me and flounced off. What a friendly lot!

I looked over at the pouting blonde. She had just asked if I was new, so I smiled and nodded to her, and said, 'Yes, I *am* new here.' I didn't offer my name as she hadn't told me hers. I was a bit wary of her, especially as no one so far had been very nice to me.

She was staring at my chest. I frowned and looked down and then back up at her.

'I thought so, haven't seen you here before. Watch out for Kelly and her mate when they come in later. I'll point them out. You've got even more of a flat chest than they have. If you end up grabbing their few reg clients they'll see you as competition … Watch out, love, I wouldn't mess with Kelly.'

I nodded my head slowly. I had no intention of messing with anyone. I looked back to the stage and mumbled 'thanks'.

Oh dear, I must have been looking all naive and shocked. People are forever telling me to watch my back, and now they were doing it here too. Well, at least it was better to know I should watch my back than to be stabbed in it, and in this dark environment I wouldn't be the slightest bit surprised if that kind of thing didn't happen all the time.

I was still looking at the stage. The busty girl was now lying on her back, splitting her legs and shoving her shaven naked crotch practically into the face of the gent seated in front of her below the stage. Did we all have to do that? I hadn't seen a girl on stage do it before, not so up close anyhow, but then again, I had spent so much time dashing to the loo on my few trial nights I wasn't often enough near the stage to see much of what the other girls were doing.

The guy who was getting the stage show up close and personal was by this point a very dark shade of beetroot and dribbling drink down his shirt. The girl on stage wasn't even looking at him but at the mirrored ceiling. Somehow she had both her hands round under her legs. From where I was standing at the side it looked like she was spreading herself open for him with her fingers.

I looked over at the blonde girl beside me. Cocking my head in the direction of the girl spreadeagled on stage, I said, 'I thought no penetration, even with fingers, was allowed? A couple-of-foot-distance council-rule thingie.'

She nodded. 'Yep,' she said, looking at the girl on stage and then back to me and shaking her head.

'She's pushing it, just showing him what she's got. No class, that one.' She wrinkled up her nose. 'The rules are very vague. She's one of *those* anyhow.' She virtually spat the words out.

I must have been staring at her blankly. One of *those*? A stripper? A porn star? A contortionist? I must have looked really confused.

The blonde just nodded back at the girl on stage, who was now on all fours with her bum in Mr Beetroot's face, wiggling about like she was having some kind of fit – either that or she was covered in invisible ants.

'You know ... one of *them*! One of the girls who give their number out to guys and go off with them after working here ... You know, the girls who say they are dancers but are actually whores. You can always tell 'em – they dress really trashy and simulate sex rather than actually dancing ...' She went on and on in disgust. I just listened while watching the stage show paid for by Mr Beetroot.

OK, I thought. On reflection, I don't think Miss Priss should be the one to ask how I would go about getting extra, after-work clients, or how I would slip them my number without anyone noticing, for that matter. She droned on in my ear as a mental barrier 'CAREFUL WHAT YOU SAY TO THIS ONE' went up faster than Mr Beetroot's erection in the front row.

On the plus side, Miss Priss here can't have thought I looked like a whore. Which had to be good – I hoped.

'See, I know you're not one because you're dressed elegantly and you're not wearing the cheap platform plastic shoes they always do.' She looked me over very intently. 'So where did you work before?'

Oh no. Thoughts were running round and round in my head. I didn't think this girl knew what she was talking about or what I was planning to do, but maybe I was wrong? Maybe she had clocked me and was digging?

I have worked with lots of whores, and only one wore the nasty, ugly plastic stripper shoes Miss Priss was talking about, and that was Suzie, the amateur porn star who worked in brothels on the side – but then again, she *was* a stripper.

I just shook my head. 'Nowhere, I haven't danced before at all.'

I thought telling a little bit of the truth was better than telling a lie. And maybe I'd be able to squeeze other information out of Miss Priss here if she thought I was green and needed her help.

'Look, some guys have just come in. Let's team up and go and say hello.' She sauntered over to two City types in suits, and I tagged behind, putting on my best smile.

'Fancy a dance, gents?' She sidled up to them with a killer-watt smile.

No, they didn't, and neither did the next group of men that came in; they all looked like they needed some Dutch courage before they could ask a woman to strip for them. Either that or two girls approaching them when they had just walked in was a bit intimidating. My new companion in charm Miss Priss made her excuses and suggested that maybe we should split up, as asking the guys if they wanted a dance might be easier to do separately. With that she slunk off to the loos, to 'refresh', as she put it.

I had more luck when she left me to it. Approaching an older gent who was sipping some dark liquid at the bar, I felt more confident than I had.

'Excuse me, can you tell me what the time is?' I queried, tapping him on the arm.

'Sure. It's 9.40 p.m., honey,' he said, looking me over as I thanked him and asked, 'I don't suppose you want a lap dance?'

'OK,' he agreed, 'but just a £5 one down to your underwear. Too much off, and I'll have a heart attack, my love,' he whispered in my ear as we found a table off to the side away from the bar for me to dance for him. At least it was only down to my lingerie. It wasn't being naked that bothered me, but a naked dance had to be done on the big, shiny stage, which could be seen throughout the club and drew most of the men's attention. What if I fell off! Now that *would* be embarrassing.

I was bound to have to do a naked dance some time but as I started slowly wiggling about to the music I pushed it to the back of my mind. Sliding my dress off slowly for half a pop song I didn't even recognize was easy – I had done that before – and in a dark corner with only one set of eyes on me it was no big deal. It was the stepping out of the dress that was difficult. How do you stop a clingy dress pooling round your ankles like a fabric boa constrictor trying to trip you up and wrap itself around your heels? Next time, I suppose I could always lift it over my head, as the girl across the room was now doing in her shadowy corner.

The man sipped his drink. I wasn't paying much attention to him. As I was dancing around him in my black bra, knickers and hold-up stockings, I was still thinking of the other girl who was dancing. Why hadn't I thought of that? Dress over head, genius! Unwrapping would be better, but I couldn't remember the last time I had seen a sexy wrap dress for sale anywhere. Knowing me, next time I danced and tried pulling my dress over my head I would get it caught in my earrings and nearly take an ear off.

The old man held out a £5 note at the end of the song and said thanks as he got up to resume his place at the bar. I hurried to get dressed, tucked the note in my stocking top and started looking for my next paying spectator. Fingers crossed the night would go as fast as that last dance had gone.

A rowdy group of men had come in a few minutes earlier. I had noticed them out of the corner of my eye as I was dancing for my £5 client. They had virtually been jumped on by some of the girls who had just sprung from the changing room. The rowdy men had fended them off

7

until they had settled at a big table near the stage, and now one of the men was gesturing me over, as I was close by from my previous dance. That was handy.

Nodding in his direction, I adjusted my dress and joined their group. I said hi to them, and to two other ladies who were already seated chatting to two of the men at the end. I hadn't seen them come in. They sat there at the end of the huddle of men, talking animatedly, and didn't even acknowledge me. Fine, they weren't the ones who were paying anyhow. I was still trying to pick up the etiquette. How did it all work? No one spoke about it. The girls couldn't all be this unhelpful, surely? Even a whorehouse was friendlier than this. The tall man at the end of the table, who was talking to a stunning brunette, was a groom, I gathered, out on his stag night. I smiled as one of the men handed me a £10 note and gestured over the chatter of the excited group to a nearby table by the stage.

Oh dear. £10 meant a nude dance up on the stage. OK, I reasoned with myself, it was only three feet off the ground and the stage was vast – it wasn't as if there was really any danger of me falling off. As we made our way to a front-of-stage seat, I looked over to the two girls on stage dancing. They were not completely naked, which was a relief. It meant they had been paid to stay on stage for at least two songs, so during at least the start of the next song I would not be the only one up there – or I hoped not. I veered off to the side to seat my Mr £10, close to where I was aiming to dance. There was no way I was going to dance at the front of the stage under that strong spotlight – not that the side looked any less bright. OK, deep breath: how bad could this be?

I couldn't see him, but the DJ must have been having a laugh – how can a white girl strip to up-tempo reggae? Idiot. Wasn't there a song about shooting the DJ? Neither of the other girls looked bothered. They just carried on, wiggling away, both of them out of time, and now naked. Any more deep breaths and I was going to look like an inflatable doll. Pull yourself together and get on with it, I whispered to myself. Oh, and smile. With that, and having made it up the steep side steps without tripping over my hem, I sauntered to the spot where my eager Mr £10 was sitting and started to move in time to the music.

Most of the men were looking goggle-eyed at the busty girl I had seen 'dancing' earlier, who was still spreading her legs, now for a different beetroot-faced man on the other side of the dark stage. Good. At least most of the attention would be focused on her. With the lights in my face I could hardly see the rest of the room, so I concentrated on looking at the man seated below me and cut off the rest of the crowd, as if they were not there.

Now even I was dancing out of time, like the other girls. I could feel the music more than hear it as the blood rushed in my ears and blocked out most of the sound.

I stared at the man's nose so as to have something to focus on, and that made it easier. He gulped as I stripped off to the music as slowly as I dared. I nearly tripped myself up, pulling my dress down without thinking.

OK, must make a mental note: over my head, over my head, over my head.

I wriggled out of my knickers but kept my stockings on as they held what little money I had earned so far. I lingered so long over my knickers, I wouldn't have had time to take my hold-ups off in any case. I just managed to get naked before the song ended, quickly whipping off my bra. Ta-dah! I had done it. I was so relieved. The music had ended too quickly, though, much sooner than I thought it would.

The man I was dancing for didn't seem to mind in the least. Mr £10 had appreciated it, and his friends at the table clapped and cheered as he stood up and handed me the money. I slid it into the top of my hold-up, next to the £5 already there. From the patting on the back he got from his mates and the huge grin plastered all over his red face, I think I did fairly well for a first attempt, so I was pleased with myself, and with the fact that I hadn't fallen off either my high heels or the stage, or tripped over my dress – well, I hadn't *really* fallen; stumbling doesn't count. I quickly got off the stage, scooping up my things as I went so I could get dressed at the bottom of the steps at the side, out of the bright lights. But where had my bra gone? I was soon on my knees, hunting for it under a table in the darkness of the front row where I thought I had thrown it. I looked up when I noticed a pair of heels in front of me. My gaze climbed up Miss Priss's legs. My errant bra was swinging from her finger.

'Best to keep your stuff all in one pile on the stage when you take it off, it's easier to find at the end,' she said, handing my bra back to me. 'Why don't you introduce me?' she said, beginning to saunter over in the direction of the man I had just danced for. I managed to catch up with her while at the same time fixing my bra back on and pulling my dress on over it.

I introduced her – not that she needed much of an introduction, as she had got there first and had already said hi and was chatting to the men on the stag night. Ah, so that's how it was done, then? You made brief friends with a girl, and then, as long as you were introduced by her, gate-crashing into a group wasn't so bad. I could see where she was coming from. I needed to make more acquaintances among the girls, then, even if they were only passing ones.

She winked at me as I got a dance with Mr Back-Patter, the one who had congratulated my earlier stage-dancing observer Mr £10 when he had got back to his seat. Mr Back-Patter gave me £20 to dance for two songs for him on stage; I was to 'show him some "ass",' as he put it. I had no idea what he meant, but I had danced once now; the second time had to be a piece of cake. I walked him to the same seat, still vacant from when Mr £10 had sat in it, at the same time as a few other girls were making their way towards the stage ready for the next song, also with men in tow.

I started to dance around near the edge of the stage. I didn't have much of a choice anyway: the stage was big, but six ladies getting naked creates a whirlwind of scattered underwear you need to avoid getting tangled up in, not to mention having to keep well clear of dancing legs ending in killer pointy heels and heavy platform soles. I could see why some of the clubs had separate podiums. I lifted my dress and wriggled my bum in the man's eager face. At least this way I didn't have to look at him drooling in his beer and giving a commentary of 'Oh yes, little girl, work that ass,' and it was easier not facing towards the crowd. It also hid the fact that I winced when I raised my dress over my head: I had caught my hair in my watch strap and had to pull it free, leaving a big chunk hanging from my wrist, which I didn't notice until I left the stage. There was no way Mr Back-Patter had noticed, as he was still intently staring at my bum, and was even more goggle-eyed when I slid my thong down my legs and spread them wide to give him a good view.

Miss Priss was soon up next to me when the second song started, doing the same thing for two more tracks for one of the other men. She was halfway through and making an average job of it as I dressed at the back of the stage from my pile of discarded clothing, the majority of the gyrating, half-naked and fully nude girls still on stage.

As I wandered back to the crowd on the stag do, I felt that it was going to be a long night. No one wanted another dance or was willing to pay me to sit and chat with them.

I went back to the dressing cubby-hole to reapply my lipgloss and gather my thoughts. A lot more girls had arrived by now, and a few were quite pushy with the customers, which I didn't think would work – until it started looking like they were the ones who got the guys to pay for dances. I didn't know if I could be that pushy or aggressive; after all, all the money I had earned in the past had been by being nice. For me, a friendly smile worked to put men at ease, but it didn't look as if it was going to work too well here.

I thought to myself, Just take a deep breath, it will be over soon: it isn't too bad. As I was walking out of the dressing room a girl pushed past me in the doorway in a rush to fix a run in her stocking. I took another deep breath and looked around the main room of the club, making my way towards the bar, where there were a few men sitting on their own. I approached some of them. All of them looked me up and down and said no thanks. That was a bit disheartening. One even looked over my shoulder and said, 'No, thanks, but can you ask her to come over and say hi,' pointing to the busty girl who had pushed past me on her way into the dressing room earlier. I went up to her and said there was a guy at the bar who wanted her, and off she went to say hi, without so much as a thanks in my direction.

But even the men who were turning me down were more friendly than the girls milling around who I was supposedly working with. Fighting for the chance to dance wasn't so much dog eat dog, it was more cat eat cat. I managed to get a few more lap dances down to my undies, after asking most of the men who had come into the club, some of them twice. This went on until a regular at the club asked me to sit and have a drink with him for an hour, paying me to sit and chat, and then he asked for a stage dance. I was beginning to work out that this was the best way to earn, as it paid more. I hadn't made much money, and after having paid the house fee of £40 when I signed in that evening and parking costs, it didn't come to half as much as I had earned in a shift in the brothel.

And it wasn't getting any easier, vying with the bustier girls to dance for drunk men who kept trying for a sneaky feel when you were off guard. It didn't come easily to me, not after the straightforward clients I had normally. I had expected the club to be full of men who would ask me to dance for them; I hadn't expected to have to hustle to get them to show even the slightest interest. Unlike the brothel where I had worked, where friendliness, a fit body and skill with it got you work, in a stripclub it was all about the way you looked, and to me it seemed as if it was the girls with big boobs who grabbed the attention and got the dances. It was all about your body and nothing about physical skill. Girls who couldn't even dance in time to the music got work if they looked good. In a brothel, if a girl couldn't do the job, no matter how she looked, she wouldn't earn as much as one who did it well. There wouldn't be much work for *this* small-breasted dancer unless I hardened up and got a bit more assertive and dirty. It was dawning on me that maybe this wasn't for me, and that it really wasn't as easy as people said or thought it was.

It was now 2.15 a.m. and most of the men had left. The music had been turned off and the house lights were on. It was closing time. As I got dressed in my jeans and top to leave, wrapping my smart jacket around me, I noticed that I smelled of smoke and stale booze. My hair stank and I couldn't wait to get home and have a shower. Miss Priss had already left, without even so much as a 'see ya'. I walked out of the back door into a dark alley with a few of the other girls who were also leaving, all of them holding hulking big rucksacks and holdalls. They looked less like the glam girls I had seen earlier on stage and more like they were on their way to the gym or the laundrette.

A short dark-haired guy I had seen in the club was

outside smoking and he waved to three of the girls as they made their way up the alley. I wasn't sure who he was but I didn't feel he posed a threat; he looked pretty laidback. He nodded to me as I went by. I peeled off to the right.

'You looking for a cab, new girl?' I smiled to him and said no, it was fine, I was driving. 'I'll walk you' was his reply. It was more of a statement than an offer. Before I even had time to think or ask him if he was security for the club I heard 'Wait up' being called from behind, and two girls strode up behind us hauling big bags.

'Chio, aren't you going to wait for us, too?' A tall girl with black curly hair and big spangly earrings trotted up, the other girl at her side.

'Hi, I'm Kelly, and this is Kiki.' The two girls smiled, and Kiki, the taller of the two, put her arm around Chio, the guy in the black suit who had offered to walk me to my car. 'So, sugar, what happened to Annie?' she questioned him.

'Annie? Oh her? She broke my heart and went back to Oz last week. Why? You looking to replace her?' He winked at Kiki, who punched him lightly on the arm.

'Anyhow, you girls don't need me to look after you. I was walking the new girl here to her car, see her safe.'

'Who says we want you to walk us? The new girl might have needed us for protection against you,' joked Kelly, hooking her arm in mine.

They were being nice, but Miss Priss had warned me about a Kelly, and that was enough to put me on my guard. I didn't know who to trust; it wasn't as if Miss Priss had offered to walk me to my car.

I smiled and listened to their banter and introduced

myself. Kelly slowed down, so we were lagging behind, and I took the opportunity as we walked up the alley to the parking area at the end to ask her who the suit was.

'Oh him, he's the boss's son. He manages the club while his old man is away. Always on the look-out for a good time that one, was head over heels with Annie, a tall Australian girl, and more so when he found out she did anal. He likes a tight ass, so I hear.' She just looked at me after whispering that, gauging my reaction I guessed.

'Really' was all I said, leaving her to natter away. We caught up with the other two, and they all waved me off, saying they would see me the next day. I went to pay my ticket so I could exit the car park. I had no idea where they were going, I didn't think to ask, but both the girls went off down another street arm in arm with the owner's son.

I was exhausted when I got back home. Claudia, a Russian girl, was renting out the spare room in her flat and I had moved in a few days ago. The door to her bedroom was closed. I hadn't seen her since the other morning, when she had dashed off to an English language class she was well past needing without so much as a goodbye. She had looked very smart in a nicely pressed suit and a pair of her precious Bally shoes, which were usually all lined up in a neat row by the front door. When I moved in I had been told rather than asked not to leave my shoes next to them, as it would make them look untidy. That put me in my place.

I was so tired I couldn't think straight. I would have to wait until morning to evaluate all that had happened that evening. I had got a bit lost around the London backroads on my way home, not knowing my way very well, so it had taken longer than I thought it would. Now, I couldn't even be bothered to take my money out of my bag, tally it down in my little black book and put it in my locked box. I just flopped down on the mattress that was serving as my bed in my small, poky bedroom, curled up and fell asleep.

In the morning, when I woke up, I was vaguely conscious of Claudia stumbling around fixing breakfast. Ouch, the daylight was bright. I had only just moved in and hadn't even put curtains up in my room yet. There were bags of my stuff all around and somewhere in the mess I knew there was a pair of curtains that matched the duvet I was wrapped up in. I dragged myself out of my pit in search of the coffee I could smell next door in the kitchen.

'Morning.' I rubbed my eyes, gazing up at dressed, washed and nicely smelling Claudia.

'Morning.' She sniffed at me. 'You smell discust-in!' she said, wrinkling up her nose. With some toast in one hand and a cup in the other, she walked past me into the sparsely furnished lounge and plonked herself down on the curving corner sofa.

'Yes, got in late last night. Just fell asleep,' I called after her. The flat was so small you could hear someone talking from one end of it to the other, and I was babbling as I emptied the boiling water from the kettle into a mug that I had found in the cupboard. 'You weren't at the club last night?' I queried, searching for the sugar, to go with the coffee, which I had unearthed in a tin.

'No' was all I got back, as I heard the TV go on in the

lounge. So much for a sociable flatmate. Maybe she was like Layla, my ex-flatmate, who never fully woke up until she had had her coffee fix. But no, that wasn't it; Claudia wasn't any more forthcoming when I sat down with my coffee: black. I mentioned that there was nothing but tofu and salad in the fridge, and that she was out of milk, to which Claudia said, 'Yah, full of food,' adding that I could have the bottom shelf if I wanted. Very gracious of her, I thought, especially considering it was a five-shelf fridge and that, even with the spattering of her half-eaten food, it was nearly empty. We chatted briefly as I sipped my coffee but not about anything much.

Claudia was having some time off from working at the gentlemen's club where I had just started, but it was through the club that I came to be living with her. The day manager who interviewed me had given me her number, as she knew Claudia was looking for a flatmate. Claudia was taking a bit of a break, not to study or go away on holiday but to work for a different one, to see how it was, she said. She was going to start the following week; she 'needed a change'. Well, I suppose it was good for me – at least I would only have to put up with the moody cow at home and not at work too. Maybe if I baked her something, that would cheer her up? It had always done the trick with Layla and Sanita in my old flat – but I only had to give brief thought to how you can make a pie out of tofu before I disregarded that idea.

Claudia got up, claiming she had to meet her man for lunch, and was off in a puff of expensive perfume. I wasn't sure I was warming to her; she was a bit cold, snobby and up herself, the way she looked down at me.

But hey, she *was* nearly six foot tall, she was bound to look down on short little me.

I went back to the club that night after a long morning shower, having fixed up my room a little and stocked the fridge from the supermarket down the road. I didn't care what Claudia said: a girl couldn't live on tofu alone. I had wandered from shelf to shelf in a bit of a daze. Why wasn't I enjoying the dancing job? Why was stripping considered better than being a lowly hooker? Just because you got paid for only being naked and didn't have to have sex with strangers, stripping was apparently OK. I was over-rationalizing, I knew it, but I wasn't happy and felt unsettled. I had passed a special-offer shelf twice and had put two cans of the same thing in my basket before I realized I didn't even like tinned macaroni and put them back.

After the poor money I had made on my first night, I was determined to make a go of it. There must just be a knack to it. It was bad enough that I hated every moment. What was the point in teasing men? Taking their money and then not being able to have my wicked way with them? But at the very least I should be earning enough for that not to worry me too much. I could always pick up a man for free sex if I needed it. I didn't like to think I would have to do that yet, but it was always an option.

Maybe I should ask Claudia for some tips – after all, she used to work there, too: she might have some inside knowledge that was evading me. And if I asked her advice it might make her friendlier towards me ... but I just had a deep-down feeling that she would revel in lording her knowledge over me. It wouldn't surprise me at all. I had tried to be friendly to her since I moved in, but to no avail. Wonder if a packet of Hobnobs would cheer her up more than a tofu pie?

2. *Come Again?*

'Hello, pretty one.' Chio was on the back door when I arrived, early, for work a few evenings later.

'Oh, hi.' I plastered on my cheesiest smile, hoping he hadn't noticed how disappointed I was at having my attention drawn away from the cute black security doorman who had just winked at me over a ledger on a pedestal and turning to look at him. Next to the smart-suited six-foot security guard, Chio looked nothing more than a pale, short, unappealing member of the opposite sex, and standing under one of the spotlights in the well-lit back corridor didn't do him any favours either: his thinning hair and dark eyes were even more pronounced.

I shuffled off quickly, not wanting to get caught between two sparring males, but Chio lingered, tagging along behind me as I dashed into the poky black dressing-hole. It was a far remove from the contract, or agency, strippers' fancy mirrored room down the corridor. I kept hearing about them. Their agents made sure they had the better dressing rooms, and they were also the most glam girls in the club; the others would point them out in passing. For some reason they didn't pay the house fee but they did give a cut of whatever they earned to an agent, who either sent them to different clubs each night or had them contracted to one club for a few weeks and would then transfer them to another. They were in high demand, darting around the club between men. As yet I hadn't had a chance even to catch the eye of one of them, let alone chat – if that was possible without getting a face full of tits, my head being at the same height as their cleavage.

I changed quickly and put the things I might need – really just make-up – in a small handbag. The bag was meant to be for the oodles of cash I was supposed to be making, so that all those notes tucked into the top of my stockings didn't weigh them down. Ha, that was a laugh. At least this time I had remembered to bring it with me, though, not that it was really going to hold more than lipgloss and a few well-palmed notes – if I was lucky. I clipped the bag shut and went off to stash my backpack with the vile house mother, Vera. It held all the things I probably wouldn't need but could retrieve from the locker cum cubby-hole if I did. It contained some normal clothes, a cheap coat, sensible shoes to drive in, a spare dress in case I fancied a change, and a front pocket full of plasters, hair bands and my hair brush. Nothing of value, just in case it was nicked.

Vera was in her cubby-hole when I went past, perched on a stool near the contract girls' dressing rooms reading a book, apparently not too busy. She must have been in her fifties if she was a day, and she had a cold blue stare and a mouth that hardly had a smile. Her short bleached hair was showing its roots, but she wasn't unkempt: you could see that from her gleaming long talons, which were immaculate. In smart slim-cut trousers and a blouse, her glasses on a gold chain around her neck, she held court here, looked after your bag for a tip and sold you over-priced cosmetics and stockings if you needed them. I wondered if she had ever been a stripper. It was hard to imagine it, and if she had, no one mentioned it.

Being new, there was no way I was going to ask her directly, especially as she was a bit pissed off with me. I had taken my bag from the locker cubby-hole last night when she wasn't around, not knowing she wanted a £10 'tip' for watching over it. I had got away with it the previous times because, being a new girl and a new face, she hadn't had time to register me. I hadn't stood out from the crowd, what with all the other girls milling around at the end of the night, rushing about getting ready to go home, wanting to leave as soon as they could. But last night, when she realized the bag she had watched over with countless others belonged to me, she had accosted me as I was getting dressed and demanded her tip in a rather abrupt sort of way, telling me the score, which everyone around me seemed to know but no one had bothered to mention.

No wonder a few of the other girls stacked their cheap bags and even cheaper coming-to-work clothes in the darkest corner of the dark, doorless hole of a dressing room we had to put up with as independent dancers. I didn't want to leave my stuff out in the open like that and thought the lockers would be a safer bet, but now I was on Vera's radar I thought it best to pay her upfront, and for the days I hadn't, just to make her happier with me. I assumed that house mothers at a stripclub were akin to a receptionist in a brothel: if you were nice to them, they liked you and made your life at work a little easier.

'So, anyone shown you around yet?' Chio eased his frame away from the wall as I pushed aside the curtain to come out from the mirrorless dressing room. He must have been waiting to chat some more and, due to the fact it was still early and not many girls were in, he was obviously lacking in people to talk to. Oh joy and lucky me.

'Er, sort of, thanks, yes. I'm looking for Vera?' I asked, hoping the question would give me an excuse to get away.

'Um, she's down there. I think you forgot to pay the house fee when you came in. I can't play favourites, you know, I have to write it in.' He waggled his eyebrows at me as he leaned in, talking lower now. 'Of course, if you sucked my dick for a bit . . .?'

I eased back like I hadn't understood. 'That's OK. I'll see Vera first, drop off my bag and then come and pay the fee at the back door.' I rushed past to get out of his way and to the safety of the gleaming agency dressing rooms, which had a bold sign that said 'NO MEN BEYOND THIS POINT' just outside its door. I had my fingers crossed the notice extended to the boss's son. It wasn't as if it was there for the dancers' modesty; it was more likely that it was there to stop men who had 'got lost' or to keep anyone from wandering in and stealing our bags.

Chio was making me feel really uneasy now. You expect that sort of thing from customers, but not from a manager. Maybe it sounds a bit snooty coming from a whore, no less, but I really think that a good business shouldn't involve its girls giving freebies in lieu of fees. It's just bad form. If the bosses expected it to happen and didn't see a problem in it, then that spoke volumes about

24

the way they ran their business – and it wasn't a business I really wanted to be involved in, especially as that sort of thing tends to cause a bad atmosphere. Any well-run business which looks after its girls doesn't need to do that. Madams might be bitches sometimes, but there's a lot to be said for working for one of them and not having to give freebies to a jumped-up wannabe pimp.

And things weren't getting any better moneywise. That night, I did a few dances on stage, which made up for the money I had given to Vera for looking after my bag, an expense I hadn't expected to have to cover in addition to the house fee and the cost of parking. I had to do quite a few dances just to break even as it was. The evening dragged on. The club was busier but there were more men drinking the overpriced drinks than wanting to pay for dances.

The end of the night came as a relief, especially as I had to deal with a drunk. I did a lap dance for him and he wasn't happy about the fact that I hadn't fully stripped, so he grabbed hold of me by the waist and tried to shove his finger up through my thong for a bit of a laugh. He gurgled as I stamped on his toe with my heel until he let go. A security guard saw what was going on and, as I dashed off to the dressing room to catch my breath, he came over to have a word with the groper, who had stood up and was trying to follow me. But Security didn't throw him out as I had expected they would, even after I told them what he had done. They did keep a watch over him, just in case he did it again – which he didn't, as he was now far too drunk to do pretty much anything at all. I just stayed over at the other side of the club, away from him, trying to smile as best I could as the men got drunker, the smoke got thicker and hands took any opportunity they could to touch and grope.

I didn't feel well at all, a bit dizzy, as I hadn't eaten as much as I should have before I came to work, and I didn't have a snack bar in my bag, which I usually did. I could really have done with a cup of tea too at that point, but the club didn't do coffee, let alone tea. I had chewing gum on my shoe, my hair smelled of stale smoke and all the men ogling me had either bad breath or body odour. It was obnoxious having to dance around them so close. Why was it that I was doing this again? Oh yes, the money – that was it.

Well, I reasoned, it can only get easier. The club was full to bursting with people, but my purse didn't fill up anywhere near as much as I wanted it to. The novelty of having to hustle for money was wearing thin, and the loud music was pulsing through my head and giving me a splitting headache. You had to shout to be heard over it.

At last it was over. It felt good to get back to the flat and, after a long shower, my headache had subsided enough for me to fall asleep as soon as my head hit the pillow. If Claudia came back that night I didn't hear her and, as I slept until noon, I didn't see her for the rest of the day either, which was annoying, as I wanted to ask her how she managed to avoid the drunken late-night gropers.

A week later, and the money I was earning at the club was still not as good as I thought it would be. I was sticking it out – I am not a girl to give up *that* easy: I wasn't going to leave just yet. The money *had* to get better. I hadn't really known what to expect, but I had been reckoning on at least £100 clear, if not more, per evening, and I was averaging £60–£80 if I was lucky. Even when I made a real effort to be friendly to the customers, they didn't want me to dance for them. It wasn't just me, though. Most of the girls at the club were complaining, grumbling that there were a lot of girls on shift and not enough men coming in to give them all enough work during the week. New girls would appear every night to give it a go, never to be seen again. I guess they thought the money would be better than it was, like I had.

And there were so many extra costs on top: house fees, house mother fees, car parking . . . If a man paid by credit card the club took 3 per cent as a transaction fee; even if he paid for a dance with the 'house paper money', which he was overcharged for in any case, we still got £2 less cashing it in at the end of the night. Another transaction fee, so the cashier said. Ironically, in a way I felt I was screwed more working in a stripclub than I had ever been in a whorehouse!

I had tried to make friends with a few girls, but as soon as I did they would leave or begin to get snotty, so I stopped trying. It was the hugely busty women who were the high earners at dancing, and I found I could earn more by sitting and chatting with the men and getting them to order overpriced drinks. Men were always asking me out after hours, but they didn't realize how late we worked; we had to stay until the end of the shift. Even if they were OK with you saying, 'Sure, I can meet you, say, after 2 a.m., I can't leave this moment,' as soon as

I mentioned what I thought was a suitable price, of around £150 for an hour, they tended to walk, saying it was too much. From what I heard from the other girls' chatter £150 was low compared to the high-priced girls working in London they had heard of. No one claimed to know any personally, though, which was frustrating.

There was no way I was going to take such a risk for less money. Just because you could get a nude stage dance for a tenner, for some reason men expected that £100 would secure you for the entire night – mind you, most were so drunk by that point I shouldn't have expected them to be thinking clearly. As yet, I hadn't been able to pick up any after-hours work and, what with the inebriated state of most of the men in the club by the end of the night, I wasn't sure I really wanted any, despite the fact that my funds were running low. After paying to park my car in central London during the day, and for rent and other costs, it didn't look like I was going to save as much as I was used to saving.

And Claudia, my so-called flat 'mate', wasn't much help when I asked her for any tips she might have for stripping. She just looked me over and said, 'Darling, you're short and have no boobs – of course you won't earn that much. If you were as pretty and tall as me, you might have a chance.' And with that she pranced off for lunch. I just smiled, all the while thinking, You bitch. At least steering clear of her in the flat wasn't hard to do: she was never there.

'Hello, hun.' I called Layla, in need of a sympathetic ear to rant into. She was about the only one I could talk to about this stuff, and I explained my issues with the club, how it wasn't as good as I thought it would be and how unhelpful my new flatmate was.

'Sod blooming Claudia. You're not as tall as her – so what? – and you shouldn't make your boobs bigger just for that, that's daft. What about saunas in the area? Why not stick to something you're better at?'

We chatted for what seemed an age. The idea of working in a sauna had run through my mind a few nights before, when the drunken bloke had groped me. I'd thought, I used to get paid better for that sort of thing, and putting up with this was just going backwards.

'I could get a boob job. Lots of girls at the club have had it done, and theirs turned out OK.' I had been toying with the idea, but Layla was horrified. I could hear it in her voice.

'There is nothing wrong with you,' she tutted on the other end of the line. 'You want to look like some silicone Barbie, or what? They always just look real fake.'

We chatted some more and I brushed off the surgery option after having spoken to her. Maybe she was right about looking for another sauna to work for, in London. Finding out if that would pay more would be a better option than having a boob job just to be able to earn more at the club. I could always do short shifts at both until I worked out which was better. I was missing sex, but the money was also a big issue. And there had to be places like the one I worked for before here in London.

Layla didn't have a clue where to start searching, and neither did I. I had only been in London a few weeks and still hardly knew anyone except Claudia. I wasn't going to ask the girls at the club, that was for sure; I didn't know if I could trust any of them. And, after Claudia's useless advice about how to earn more money, I really didn't think she would be much help.

3. Knocking Shops

'So, how's the club you're working at?' I asked. I hadn't seen Claudia in days. I had no idea where she had been, I didn't much care, so I didn't bother to ask. She had been coming back to the flat later than I had, after work when I was tucked up asleep, and then she'd be up and gone before I surfaced. Whenever she was back and around in the evenings, she flounced off to bed before I could speak to her.

It was a Saturday, and I had wandered into the lounge. Saturday was one of Claudia's days off, or so she mumbled. She didn't need to go to her English language class either, so she was lolling around the flat with a mudpack on her face and her brown, bobbed hair tied back out of the way.

'New club? It OK.' She looked up from her fashion mag. 'Why? You not make it work at the club?'

'No, not really. If it was that good, you would have stayed, surely?' I quizzed her.

'It very good, but my man pay me not to dance there any more, he not want me to dance, so I dance somewhere he not know.' She looked terribly pleased with herself.

'Oh, how do you get away with still dancing then?' I sat down next to her with my tea.

'He thinks I have night classes now. Really, my

31

morning classes very short so all good. I can dance at night instead.' She looked happier than I had seen her before. 'He taking me shopping today for more shoes. I meet him for lunch every day. Can you not be here at one? He is picking me up.' She was positively beaming now. 'He thinks I live here alone.' It seemed the shortest path to Claudia's heart was to buy her shoes for her big feet.

'Sure, I'm going out anyhow, to look for some saunas or massage parlours to work at as well as dancing.' I took a sip of tea and watched her expression.

She didn't look that perturbed. 'You have massage certificate? My friend, she does that. She find places in the back of the free paper.' She riffled through a few papers stacked beside the sofa and thrust one at me. ''Ere, you probably do better there than club. My friend, she too short to dance too, she do well give massage.'

I smiled and thanked her for the paper, but I couldn't work out what being short had to do with not being able to dance. I had seen lots of shorter albeit bustier girls in the club make a packet. I had a feeling Claudia wasn't the most clued-up girl on the planet, despite the world we both worked in, and I just knew she had no idea what really went on in a massage parlour or sauna.

'OK, I am off to beauty parlour. I need a pedicure before I go shopping.' Off she strutted to get ready, leaving me to pore over the free London paper for ads in the back. There was only one in the job section advertising for masseuses, and it was asking for certificated women only, which made me wonder if it was a proper massage place rather than a massage parlour, which was

London's equivalent to a brothel in the outer counties. The description in the ad sounded a bit brief and dodgy for it to be a legit massage place, but I was still not too sure.

I went through the other papers and circled any of the massage and sauna ads that looked any good, hoping that an expensive ad would mean an expensive place, one that I could call and ask if they needed any girls. I called five from the paper, and only three picked up. I was briskly given a time to come for an interview. I drew stars against the ones that said, 'Turn up for an interview and we will put you to work.' Only one of the three asked if I had a certificate, and when I said I didn't, the older woman on the other end of the line said it didn't matter and to come anyway, they would sort it out.

All I had to do was wait until I had a day off from dancing to go and check them out, do an interview and see if I wanted to work at any of them.

I drove to the first one on my list two days later, spurred on by still not earning well at the club. It wasn't going any better than it had been; the men were still drunken assholes with wandering fingers who didn't ask or pay. I was really missing the way I used to work.

When I got to the first sauna, I didn't even bother to go up to the door, let alone to knock. It was down an alley and looked decrepit, paint peeling off the door and ripped, dirty curtains in the upper windows. I didn't get a good impression at all, so what would a punter think if he came to call? If he truly wasn't bothered about the state of the place, would he really be someone I would want to meet? Probably not.

The next sauna on my list seemed more promising. It had had one of the smarter ads in the free paper and, from the outside at least, it looked clean. After being buzzed in, I descended to a white, strip-lighted corridor and then walked along it towards a heavy, metal-grilled door. A door on the other side of it swung inward. Now, beyond the bars of the grille, I could see a security guard, who filled most of the doorway behind, and he could see me. Apparently, little me didn't look like much of a threat, because he unlocked the door and ushered me in with a grunt. I was glad I had told Layla where I was going. She was calling me back in ten minutes. The door didn't look as if it was there to keep the girls in; it was more to protect the girls from people trying to get in. And by the look of the bootmarks on the outside doorframe, it seemed that someone had wanted to get in and hadn't been too happy about being locked out.

The disinterested, rough-looking door guard showed me in to a white-tiled reception room and plonked his ample frame back down on his stool, picking up the paper that he had discarded to let me in.

Inside, the place looked a bit worn. It was dotted with cheap plastic patio chairs and tables, and there were a few women draped either over the chairs with their feet up on another or sitting round a table sharing a fag while playing cards, wearing identical grubby lab-coat wraps which had once been white.

The ladies didn't look unhappy; they just wore the bored expressions I had seen before in the faces of other working girls I had come across in the past – the tired expression you had after a long, slow day with little custom.

Some looked up with a smile as I entered, but seeing that I was another woman, who might add to their number, and not a client, the smiles dropped. Uninterested, they went back to their cards, to filing their nails, reading their magazines or watching the caged TV high up on the wall in the corner, its remote control hanging off a chain attached beside it.

The room was whitish and, from what I could see as I stood at the tall counter on the right, it led into a corridor with curtained doorways all along it. One of the white-robed women, who was sitting on a stool at the counter and looked the same as the rest but a bit older and of a happier nature, beckoned me over. I said hi and that I had phoned a couple of days ago for an interview, and she nodded and hopped off her stool, coming around the counter to invite me to sit down for a chat on one of the vacant plastic garden chairs by a wobbly table. I was feeling very uneasy.

The guard on the door was just sitting on his stool reading his paper. He looked a bit miffed when he was interrupted again to open the door for one of the girls, who grabbed her coat and bag and said she was going out for fags and would be back in ten minutes.

I had been right: he wasn't there to keep the girls from escaping; he was just a doorman for their security should they need him. The tired-looking girls didn't even look up from their lounging or TV-watching.

I asked a few questions about the security and was told that it was OK, that it was all very safe and the late-night drunks were dealt with well, as an extra security guard came on shift in the evening.

The fact that they needed two big security guards and a barred door didn't make me feel secure at all. I wasn't surprised though the environment was putting *me* on my guard, so I don't know what it did for the visiting men who, when they were buzzed in, were asked to look at the seated women, pick one, pay the cashier (as my interviewer called herself) and go off to one of the tiny, curtained rooms equipped with a massage bench for thirty minutes.

It became clear that you had to barter with the client in the room yourself to get any money from him for other services, as the fee that was paid to the cashier was the entrance and room fee only. And it didn't cover security, I was told, so both of the guards were given £10 each by every girl who was on shift as a kind of tip. There were no showers and only one toilet on the premises. When I asked where the kitchen was the cashier looked at me strangely and told me that all the girls brought their own food for the whole of the day or ordered take-outs. At that point I left, saying that I would call for a shift, even though I had no intention of doing so; I just wanted to leave.

The atmosphere there was not what I was used to from the other place I had worked in. For a start, I didn't like the idea of having to barter with the men. I already knew I wasn't very good at it, and I would probably end up as miserable as one of the women sitting on the plastic chairs.

*

After these two disappointing parlour hunts, I made a list of a few addresses and drove around the city to check them out during the day, when I wasn't at the club dancing. I thought I'd try and find one that looked better than all the grimy others before wasting time and calling for an interview. In the middle of the week I found a sauna in a part of east London that was smarter than the area the others had been in, with a classy black door with a shiny canopy over it. It looked ten times better than the five saunas and massage parlours I had found closer to where I lived, and the dingy one I had gone to for an interview. From the outside, at least, it looked like it might be one of the better ones in London. The fact that its ad, in the free paper, which I had realized you could pick up outside tube stations, was one of the bigger, flashier ones was also a good sign. Basically, the bigger and more expensive the ads, the larger and more prosperous the parlour, which meant the business was better run and, all in all, it would be a good place to work. Some of the girls I'd worked with the year before, I remembered, had mentioned this logic, and indeed that was how they had found the brothel we were all working in back then and why they had called it for an interview in the first place. The places at the bottom of the scale tried to get away with a brief couple of lines in their ads, and that just showed how small and cheap they really were.

I hung around for a while on the other side of the street, watching to see if anyone came in or out. After half an hour, with no one showing, I gave up. I didn't really know what I was looking for but at least it had given me a good feel for the area. I drove back to the flat in Holborn to get ready for my night shift at the gentlemen's club. When I got back I called the sauna I had just visited to see if they needed any girls and was told, yes, they did, as they had just opened a couple of months back. Could I come in the next afternoon? Of course I was more than happy to, especially since the girl on the other end of the phone sounded friendly, not as harsh as most I had tried to speak to so far. Most of the receptionists I had called to ask for information had dry, rasping voices which sounded suspicious as to why a woman was calling. Talking to the receptionists gave a good indication of what a man would hear if he called. I hedged on the fact that this sauna would be busy because of the way the receptionist sounded.

My interview turned out not to be all that taxing, just a few questions, and the atmosphere most certainly was not as depressing as its 'plastic-chair prison' brother which I'd visited the week before. The receptionist was small, pretty and blonde. Her name was Emma, and she looked around my age. She was more interested in when I could start than in asking about any massage certificate I might have or even for my national insurance number (not that I would have given her the real one), both of which most receptionists had asked about even over the phone.

Emma said that the boss would be coming in later that afternoon if I wanted to sit with the other girls and wait to have a chat. I nodded; I thought it would be a good idea to have a look around and sit with the other three girls, just to see what the atmosphere was really like. The other room was separated from this one only by a swing saloon door, and I had spotted the girls milling around behind it while I was sitting at the desk speaking to Emma. She introduced me to the girls as Shelly, which we had just chosen from a list of names.

I had come up with the names I had used before, and she then went through a list in a folder of girls they had working or who had worked for them to make sure that there wouldn't be a clash. They didn't want to have two girls working there with the same name; Emma said it would be far too confusing for everyone. Shelly was her suggestion. She had rejected the three I had thought up, all beginning with S. I didn't particularly like the name but we settled on it, and so Shelly it was. Who knew I looked like a Shelly?

Emma asked one of the girls to show me around and then dashed off to answer the phone.

Although this place was better than the last one I'd been to see, it was still nothing like the one I'd worked at the year before, which was pretty opulent, with proper beds. As I found out from the girl showing me around, the workrooms in this London sauna were pretty much similar to all the others in London, it didn't matter where you went. They were set out with proper fold-out massage beds, like the ones you'd get in a rather grotty back-street physio's. Apparently, in London, proper beds with a mattress would automatically flag the sauna as a brothel and it would be shut down. As it was, if the council did any checks that fire and safety requirements were being met, this place would pass as a sauna and, as such, get a safety certificate so they could operate under local council regulations. Most places proudly hung the certificate in a prominent place on a wall, mostly so that men would think it was something to do with how 'safe' the girls who worked there were. The receptionists would even use the fact that they had a safety certificate from the council as an extra selling point over the phone if men asked. All it really meant was that the place wasn't crawling with rats and that the fire exits weren't blocked. It had nothing at all to do with the staff, as all the men presumed, but if they asked if we did have a safety certificate we just told them yes and didn't bother to correct them if they had a notion that it was something else. After all, who were we to disappoint them – and our pockets?

So, as long as the place looked like a sauna and actually had a steam room, it was a sauna to the council; otherwise it would just be categorized as a lowly massage parlour like the white-tiled, plastic-chaired one I had already seen and rejected.

After being shown around, I joined the girls, who were all dressed in tight white overall dresses. They perched on a thin, padded bench attached high up a wall in an alcove. It looked terribly uncomfortable, and it was if you sat there for too long, but it was the only seating in the lounge. Unless you sat up straight on the narrow bench you slid off the front and banged your knees on the table in the middle, as I found out, to the cost of my knees.

The girls were a mixed but friendly lot. A tall black girl, a small Chinese girl and a curly-haired New Zealander all looked up and smiled when I was shown in.

When I chatted with them about other places to work in the area they gave the impression that a sauna was a cut above the rest, but not in a snobby way, more in an earning potential kind of way. They made it perfectly clear that saunas were considered much more high class than massage parlours, and a brothel or smaller working flat with two girls and a maid were a step down even from the massage parlours.

It was a bit confusing – after all, a working girl did practically the same thing in each one – however, having seen the places I had in London, I sort of got what they were getting at: nice places to work were few and far between. There were apparently some places where girls aspired to work, and this sauna was one of them. Or, at least for these girls it was. The next rung up was a massage-certificated sauna, and you had to know someone who worked there even to get an interview, and that was after you spent a year at an adult education college learning massage in order to get the appropriate certificate. That was what the girls were saying anyhow. I made the mistake of asking what this 'parlour' was like to work in and was immediately corrected: this wasn't one of those, and it definitely wasn't a brothel either. The cheek of it, this was a sauna! The Chinese girl who had objected looked very smug about this. The other two just raised their eyebrows and looked at her in amusement. Well, at least they had a sense of humour.

The New Zealand girl with curly brown hair was called Zora. She was surprised that I had even considered working at a parlour, let alone a brothel, with the way things were here in London. And given what she thought the brothels in London were like, and what she had probably seen in the past, I wasn't surprised at all at her reaction.

Emma kindly brought me a cup of tea. I thanked her for it and pretended to drink it to be polite. They were nice, and I'm sure the tea would have been fine, but I wasn't taking any chances with people I didn't know very well. I nursed the mug in my hands as Emma took her position back at her desk and I quizzed the others about how they managed on the narrow massage tables. I had never had to work on them before and I was fairly short, so the benches in the rooms were very high for me. No one knew if the council laid down a regulation height for a massage table. 'That is just the way they come,' I was neatly told by the tall, well-built black lady. There was a small collective giggle when I asked, 'The punter or the table?'

Trying to have sex on a massage table that's nearly five feet off the ground and only three feet wide is a tricky business, especially if you're with a fat man. Even a large, tall man would take up the whole table, so it was very precarious if you were on top, as there was nowhere to put your feet, and if he was on top you were likely to be squashed by his bulk. If the man was lying down and you climbed on top it was difficult to balance as all you had were little perches at either side of the table for your feet. If the man managed to get up on the bench and stayed still, you would just end up bouncing around on top till the deed was done – perfect if you were just giving a blow job, as you could crouch between his legs and he couldn't move a lot, so there wasn't much chance of him messing around, poking fingers where they shouldn't go. If he did he would fall off the narrow bench. Sex is far more dangerous on a rickety bench than a BJ could ever be, and you had to be creative with your positions. If you weren't careful, it was a long way to the floor, and usually it wasn't the cleanest of floors you'd ever seen either.

When the boss walked in an hour later it came as a bit of a surprise that she was a woman. For some reason, I was expecting the boss to be a man, but in strode a large, robust-looking lady. She was in her forties and was wearing a suit. Emma, the blonde girl on reception, had called me through when my new Mrs Boss arrived, to go and sit on the sofa in front reception and have a few words with the madam. She was pleasant enough but at the same time she gave off a Don't piss with me vibe. She had pretty much the same kind of attitude as my ex-madam, but this one had better-styled hair and a better manicure. I guessed that she didn't do any work herself but just popped in and sorted out any problems that arose.

She was exactly what I would expect a madam to be. It was Emma who puzzled me; she just didn't 'fit'. To me, she didn't look like a receptionist at all. I sat chatting to the madam, watching and listening to Emma confidently handle an idiot phone call. Receptionists had to deal with the front of house and were the front line in dealing with drunks. In all my experience receptionists had been older women.

Now, if Emma had been a working girl, that would have fitted, but it didn't make much sense that she was having to deal with the wankers on the phone, and to have a petite girl on the front desk who wouldn't physically be able to stand up to any late-night drunks? And it wasn't as if she was covering for an ill receptionist, as

I had already asked her that. She had laughed a little and said, no, she was working there full time. It wasn't a very well-paid job either. She was well spoken and could have got a better job elsewhere. It just didn't make sense.

But hey, what did I know? I was well spoken, fairly pretty (from what I was told to my face anyhow) and had an education. I could have got another job too – albeit a worse-paying one than being in the industry. It wasn't like I would have had to stock shelves at Tesco's; I could manage a team of people doing it, at a pinch. That was if I could have filled in the gaps of over a year on my CV. Other girls had asked in the past why I was a working girl, and I didn't have much of a reply other than the money. Maybe Emma's job paid better than I thought it did.

The madam nattered away, and said she would put me on the rota. I was told to bring a black dress for my first shift, and then she would send a woman to measure me for one of the uniforms the following week if I stayed. The uniform was a fitted white short coat-dress, very much like a proper massage outfit, save for the fact that it was low cut and showed as much cleavage as it could muster – which in my case wasn't much. It was going to cost me £37, but I wouldn't have to buy it or pay for it for a week, or unless I was actually going to stay.

With a date fixed to come back and give it a try, I left, waving to the girls. It was time to go back to the flat and get ready for another slow night at the gentlemen's club. The thought of going there was now filling me with a mix of emotions, all of them negative. I couldn't help mentally counting down the days until I could jack this dancing lark in and actually do something that seemed like second nature to me. At least I was being honest with myself now. Entertaining men can come in all sorts of guises, but my forte was definitely sexual. The sauna seemed like the answer to the boredom and disillusionment I got from the club, and let's not forget the money. It just had to be better than the 'ten cents a dance' experience – or should that have been £10 a dance I was getting? Roll on the Doris Day!

4. *Bitch Mates*

I didn't hear the front door open that morning. I was up early and waiting in the lounge for Claudia to finish in the shower so I could use it. I'd turned the TV on, so the noise of the door, which was right next to the bathroom, was masked by it and the sound of the water. The first I knew that there was someone in the flat other than my sullen flatmate and I was when she screamed and then started shouting over the noise of the shower at a person I couldn't see. I dashed to the lounge door and peered out along the corridor to where the bathroom door was.

I had been drinking my morning tea and I grabbed my empty mug to use as a defence weapon against the intruder, albeit a fairly useless one. The short Indian chap who stood in the open doorway of the bathroom, his hand on the door knob, was now being pushed out by a towel-wrapped and dripping Claudia, who was shouting what I could only guess were Russian obscenities at the mumbling man, who stood at shoulder height to her. He was now being backed up against the corridor wall.

Claudia looked pissed off rather than scared, so I lowered my mug. She was fuming and screaming, 'I don't care. Get out!' at the man, who had obviously just let himself in, as a set of keys was dangling in his free hand. He had raised his voice to protest that he needed to talk.

It caught him a bit off guard when he realized that they were not the only people in the corridor and that I was standing in the doorway to the lounge.

'Who's she?' He nodded my way. By this point, I was guessing they knew each other, but I had never seen or heard Claudia mention him before or known that anyone other than the landlord had a door key. I had asked her about the landlord before I had moved in as I'd had problems with one in the past and didn't want it to happen again.

'She's a friend. Is none of your business,' she sneered at him, while trying to push him back out of the front door.

'I am not going anywhere. You bitch. I need you, I love you,' he shouted back. She froze and started to turn red with visible anger.

It was an unusual sight, tall Claudia in the corridor barring his way, looking down on this skinny, short young man. Bellowing, 'We are over, get out, get out now!', she didn't look as if she needed any help at all. She was really angry, and I felt uncomfortable standing there, caught in an ex-lovers' tiff.

'How dare you let yourself in like that?' The two of them stood in the corridor and carried on screaming at each other for a couple more minutes as I slid unnoticed back into the lounge and closed the door behind me to muffle the argument. I heard a door slam, and just at the same time Claudia swung open the lounge door and marched in looking none best pleased.

'That was Ali. He own flat I rent. We used to date, but it over now. He too stupid to understand.' She was pacing back and forth but finally she came to a stop and stood in front of me. I sat on the sofa and listened to her rant. 'You didn't lock the door behind you when you came in this morning, did you?'

I had popped down to the corner shop for milk for my morning tea, as she had drunk the last of it the night before, and put the empty carton back in the fridge. It was true, I had unchained the door when I left, but I was sure I had locked it behind me when I came back in. I was sure I had.

'Nope. I definitely closed the door behind me. Anyhow he had keys. He probably let himself in!' She flopped down on the sofa next to me as I took a deep breath in order to keep calm. It was far too early in the morning for a shouting match.

'No! You didn't chain the door when you came back!' She was looking at me like it was the obvious thing to have done and I was stupid for not thinking to do it. I could understand chaining the door at night, but during the day too? She had never asked me to do that, and I told her so.

'Why the hell would I have chained the door after me? You never asked! I didn't know you had a stalker for an ex-boyfriend.'

She just huffed at that and flounced off to her room, slamming the door behind her. Note to self: Start looking around for another place to live.

I left a few hours early for work at the club, so that I could avoid Claudia when she emerged from her room. I left my bag in the car and had a very pleasant time looking around the shops for a new dress, a wrap one that

I wouldn't have to pull over my head and so wouldn't make my hair go all static and stand on end throughout the night. After hunting around I eventually found just the thing, and it would do for the sauna too. I made my way back to my car to stash a few bags before parking in the multistorey car park down the road from the club, ready for work.

'Ooh, I like the dress.' Vera paid me the compliment as I left my bag with her. However, I had heard her say the same thing before to a few of the other girls, time and time again during the week. I guess she worked on the principle that if a girl looked happy, she was probably going to earn well and so a nice compliment early on might be to her advantage at the end of the night: she might get a bigger than average tip from a happy, minted girl. Call me a cynic but I reckon she had picked up quick that mostly it worked to her advantage.

I was more pleased by thinking that she might assume from her experience that I might earn well that night than that she claimed to like my dress. I normally hate shopping for clothes, and all the crowds, so unless I really, really had to, I very rarely went, and certainly never to cheer myself up. Today, after the episode of Claudia and the stalking ex, I must have needed the distraction more than I thought.

The night was going well. It felt like my smile was attracting men like flies, but more likely it was the low-cut clingy dress, which did look stunning, I had to admit, and even better with the new heels I had also bought. My purse was starting to fill with £5 notes and all was right with my world. This new satin dress would pay for itself in no time at this rate.

Fuck, fuck, fuck it in a bucket of fuckery. What the hell was that? Not my new dress!

I turned around to find Kiki behind me, fag in hand, apologizing but making out that I had backed into her, when I hadn't moved at all. Well, it was a busy night and a bit crowded but it was Sod's law. I now had a big fag burn in the back of my new dress and, worst of all, with me being so white and my dress being dark blue, it really showed, and my hair wasn't long enough to cover it. My good mood was gone in a flash. I made my way back to the dressing room to change into my spare dress and put an ice cube on the nasty red blister starting to appear. It was just in between my shoulder blades so it was really hard to reach.

An hour later my back-up slinky dress had a hole in the back too.

The house mother Vera had said 'Oh dear' when I walked into the back area the first time to retrieve my bag. The second time it happened, when I was all out of dresses and I hadn't seen who did it in the crowd of bodies in the dark club, she just smirked and said that I should be more careful, shouldn't I, and that 'accidents happen'. Accidents happen, my naked arse.

I wasn't totally dense. Those two, Kelly and Kiki, definitely had it in for me. I wasn't sure when Kiki had done it, but Kelly had a very snide smirk on her face over on the other side of the room as I dashed off to the bathroom. If I had been doing better than them I could have understood. They obviously felt I was stepping on their toes and they were just being vindictive, and the worst of it was that I didn't know why. One new dress couldn't cause that much envy.

One of the professional girls gave me the best advice, which was to avoid them. She said that no one would be interested in a whiny new girl who ran to the bosses because some little thing had gone wrong; it was easier to fire her and replace her with a less accident-prone one. She was one of the nicer, more well-meaning girls I had met, but I got the gist: either I kept clear of Kelly and Kiki or I would have to leave. I wasn't even a contract girl, like she was, so, being independent, I didn't have much say.

I knew, too, that I had no hope of being a contract girl at that time. They were all good dancers and knew their way around a pole, and they were all stunning, with big hair, big make-up and even bigger boobs.

The contract girls made up the main house lap- and stage-dancers. It meant that the club had at least a set number of girls working a night who looked the part. The rest of us were just to fill in really, to make the place look busy. I didn't know that when I answered the newspaper ad; I thought all the girls had got the job through an ad in the paper too. I didn't realize you could work there in a different way. No wonder they hadn't needed much info from me when I started – I doubted I was even officially on the books.

It was starting to feel like, if you didn't have an agent, you didn't have a stripper shoe to stand on. Kiki and Kelly might not have been contract girls, but they had been working at the club longer than I had and knew all the ins and outs of how the house worked. I truly was up stripper creek without a pole.

I lurked at the back of the club for the rest of the night, avoiding Kelly and Kiki, who kept on giving me the evils. I was just waiting for the night to end, and only table-danced for a few men after that, but at least that meant I was away from the stage, where all the action was going on, away from Kelly.

Later, I was on my way to the loos when a girl came out of nowhere and 'accidentally' spilled a drink all down my front. I had seen her with Kelly before, and it was too much of a coincidence for it to have been an accident. Or was it just me getting paranoid?

As it was the end of the night, I hung out in the loos drying off until it was time to go home. I couldn't be bothered to try and plaster on a big fake smile and hustle to get a dance for a measly £5 from a drunk who would blow smoke in my face and try to grope me.

I just wasn't in the mood. I was dressed and away on the dot of closing time, before the other girls had even started to change their clothes. As I drove home I called into the office of the club on my mobile phone to say I was taking some time off. I had two days before I started at the sauna, so I thought I could give that a good go, and if I didn't like it, I always could go back to the gentlemen's club. In a week or two Kiki and Kelly would have moved on, found another target or even left. If it happened again when I went back there, I could always find another club. Claudia would know a few if I needed to ask.

I'd had it! That was it, I hadn't even earned enough to pay for my new, now-ruined dress! I might be running away from the problem and giving up too soon – I had planned in my mind to give it at least a good month or so – but I didn't care. I started to think I had been spoiled working in a brothel; I hadn't felt half as undermined working there as I did working as a stripper. Men going to a brothel went there because they knew what they wanted, they asked for me and gave me the set house fee for my time. I didn't have to handle negotiations or discuss money with them; the receptionist did all that. I didn't have to hustle men and talk them into reaching into their pockets for a few notes like I did in the strip-club. I found it demoralizing. I suppose if I didn't enjoy sex as much as I do, stripping would have been the easier option, but I did. And to add to all that I was feeling unsettled at home too – if you could call a mattress surrounded by packing boxes and bin bags full of clothes home.

I was already living with one bitch. Life was far too short to have to work with them too.

5. *Moan Sweet Home*

Sauna shift 1: 12 noon–1 a.m.

Saturday 15 August 1998

5 clients = £260 (one straight massage only, tipped £15)

– £10 receptionist's tip

– £5 cab

–£37 uniform (paid upfront)

Total = £223

Sauna shift 2: 12 noon–1 a.m.

Monday 17 August

6 clients = £275 (one straight massage, no tip; 3 no sex)

– £10 receptionist's tip

– £5 cab

– £15 straight!

Total = £245

Zora, the New Zealander, and the tall black lady, two of the girls I had chatted to when I came in for the interview, worked nearly every day and told me the score with the rates at the sauna. I soon found out that after the man had paid the entrance fee, it was up to the girls themselves to deal with money for so-called 'services' in the room. Apparently this was standard in all London saunas and massage parlours. It was a bit awkward having to deal with the money yourself, and not very professional on the part of the house, I felt. In the past it had been the job of the receptionist, but this was the way it was done here now. I guess no one thought to do it any other way, as the receptionists pretty much had their hands tied, what with councils in London being more uptight than those in other counties.

They talked me through the fees the first time, but only briefly, as they were not sure if I was going to come back. Everyone (so the girls said) charged a kind of set house fee in the rooms. It had been made up by the girls themselves, according to what they thought the other houses in the area were charging.

£10 just for a massage (£15 for a straight client who only wants a massage)

£15 girl in her underwear giving a massage

£20 for one topless massage on the client

£30 for hand relief dressed

£40 for hand relief undressed

£50 for a naked massage and hand job

£60, the same as for £50, but the client can touch and fondle the naked masseuse

£70 for a massage and a covered blow job (possibly sex, if it was a regular client you liked)

£80 for a massage and sex (possibly a covered blow job, too, if it was a regular client you liked)

£90–£100 for the works: a massage, a blow job and sex (which was what we were aiming to get)

All had to take place within half an hour of the man going into the room, and everything was to be marked on the receptionist's chart. If it took any longer, we just doubled the price, as we had to pay again for occupying the room for another half-hour. It was quite a list to remember but, for the most part, men only wanted a quickie, a cheap fuck so they could get back to the office after their lunchbreak. At that time of day you mentioned the lower prices first, as that's normally what the customer had in mind and that was their spending limit. The ones who would stay longer were usually the ones who came in the evening before going out to a nightclub or the pub; any later and they had already spent most of their money and were a bit the worse for wear to last long, or even to want to stay longer.

In general, the girls would try and get away with doing as little as they could for the money in any of the price brackets. It did vary a bit, according to what the individual girl preferred to offer or do, but it was still around £80–£100 if sex was included. The guys who came in knew the score and pretty much what they wanted. Some regulars would hassle for everything for £70 if they could get away with it and some girls, if they were desperate, would do it, but at the risk of the other girls finding out and getting pissed off with them for undercutting.

If a man was new to the area and he didn't look like he knew the score, you started out by listing the higher prices, only mentioning the lower ones if he started to look a bit taken aback. Sometimes you then had to ask how much they had with them. Zora told me it wasn't unusual for a guy to be caught out and think the £10 they paid at reception was for a massage and not just the entrance fee.

Then you had to explain to the man that the house took £15 from each girl as a room fee every time she took a room, which was true, and then you could normally get the guy to stay and at least have a half-hour massage to cover your costs rather than have him walk and ask for his money back. The girls said it didn't happen often, but if it did and the man stayed, he might come back knowing the score another time and actually punt. I didn't know if I believed that, but it was reassuring to hear.

If you had a guy that walked you were out of pocket, Zora was telling me; nice of her to give me a heads-up. I didn't think it was fair that it was all so cloak and dagger, but the other girls said that was just the way it was. You either stuck it or moved on, said Zora. She was what would be considered one of the older girls (not that, at thirty-four, she looked old at all; she could get away with saying she was twenty-six) and had worked a round of saunas in the past. I liked her; she'd even lent me her old uniform, as we were the same size. She was working at this sauna, which had been newly refurbished, as she had worked here before and had liked it better than most. It wasn't great, she admitted, confessing that it used to be the pits, but at least now the new manager was updating the decor and was fair. The updating looked to me as if it only consisted of a cleaned-up shopfront with a new black canopy, a plush reception room with large velvet sofas, a lick of paint on all the walls, some new shower curtains, and some red bulbs in the work rooms, to give 'ambiance'. As all of the five small rooms had a bath and shower as well as a massage bench, there wasn't much room to swing a condom let alone a cat. The place could have had a lot more done to it, but, so I was told, at least it was better than most in the area.

Four of the work rooms were on the top floor and were reached by a spiral metal staircase, and the fifth, larger work room, the one that was used the most, was on the ground floor next to the steam room, just past the girls' lounge alcove. The steam room was a good place to sit if it was a bit chilly and the heating was on low. It wasn't like it was used by the men who frequented the sauna. In fact, I only knew of it being used twice in all the time I was there, which was handy, as most of the time the girls used it as a small laundry room, to dry stockings and such like. They had to be swiftly removed if the boss was around, otherwise she was not best amused.

The first man who came in that day picked me, which was a bit of a surprise. Emma showed him to where we were all sitting, and he pointed at me. I felt quite un-comfortable when I got up, as I had expected that we would each go out one at a time and say hello. I hadn't expected to be confronted with a man walking in to choose as I was filing my nails and chatting to the girls. It caught me a bit off guard, but I showed him to the downstairs room. It wasn't too far along the corridor, so if I needed to shout for help, I could be heard, even with the door closed.

The man was wearing a suit and looked fairly average. He chatted away, asking my name, and saying he had £80 and wanted a BJ and a fuck, with not so much as a blush or a question. He had obviously been here before, so I didn't argue and took his money, putting it in my pocket as he stripped and hopped in the shower without me even having to ask. When he came out, I held out the towel that had been provided and he wrapped it loosely around his hips and jumped up on to the bench, lying on his front and asking for talc, not oil. After standing on my toes and giving him a brief massage, unbuttoning my uniform with one hand as I did so, I stepped away to fold my uniform over the rickety chair in the corner.

My chatty businessman had relaxed and was not so chatty now that he was squirming on his front. I pulled the chair back over to my Mr Erection so I could get up on to the bench to start a blow job and then have my wicked way with him. Time was going faster than I realized. By this time he had turned over to see what I was up to, losing his towel completely along the way and releasing his average cock. I was more concerned about not falling off the chair in my heels and undies than with the cock in front of me, which was standing up like a flag pole, impatient to be sucked. I decided to kick off my shoes. He fondled my breasts and was easing down the lace of my bra to play with my nipples, which distracted him as I straddled him, taking off my bra and slithering down him to suck on the rubber I had just taken out of my stocking top. It wasn't long before I was sitting precariously on top of him with my feet either side on the edges of the massage table. With a few strokes up and down he came. Nice, simple screw. It had been a while but at least I hadn't lost my touch.

He was pretty much an average client, like the ones I usually saw in the brothel, and was all smiles and thanks as he showered, dressed and promised to come back and see me again the next week. My first booking was over. I handed £15 to Emma on the desk after I had shown him out. He was soon replaced by another late-lunch-quickie gent, much the same as the one before, knew what he wanted. A massage, blow job and sex, for £90 this time, which was fine by me and, that being that, he was gone as soon as he had come.

I was bound to get one, but at least it was only one, a walk-in off the street who hadn't realized he would need more money to get what he really wanted. The young man was nervous, I could tell, and nearly walked, until I offered to give him a massage in my undies and stockings. I said he could wank off at the end if he wanted to, which he declined, but he did take me up on the £15 straight massage, I think more out of sympathy and feeling foolish for not knowing the score and coming in with money that wouldn't have paid a street girl, if that, than because he really wanted a massage.

They came and they went, their faces all quickly forgotten by the time I had shown them out. It's hard to remember so many faces, all seen in a gloomy red-lit room, and it didn't matter what they looked like – as long as they put out with money and cock, I was a happy working girl. It had been a good, normal working day, no hassle so far, which I had braced myself for, being new. There was nothing worse than a haggler, pervy newbie-girl hunter or a guy that wants to waste time trying to please you and holds out when you only have less than thirty minutes. A few could be like that, but they were easily dealt with by hand, which was more of a subtle indication that they needed to come because time was up, rather than that they were having trouble getting it up.

You would think most men paying for a screw would just want to get on with it, but on the whole it's rarely like that at all. Ironically, you're more likely to get a roll-on roll-off guy on a date than when he's paying you. If it was as easy as a guy wanting to pay, use you and leave, being a working girl would be so much easier than the flattery, faking and falsehoods we have to deliver to get the job done.

When men pay they in some way consider themselves to be a bit of a stud if they can please a whore. It's perverse: the men who come in the door never consider themselves average punters. Of course they are, but they think, for some reason, what with the media and what they have read, which is mostly salacious tabloid gossip, that all the men coming through the door (apart from themselves of course) are fat, ugly, desperate men that just want to fuck us and leave. And so they think that, as a working girl has sex so often, she must be hard to please and, in turn, that it must be a treat for us to be pleased first. They like to think they are special, that they're doing something nice for you and be able in their heads not to believe they are just using you. But it is actually very annoying sometimes, if they drag it out and you have to fake it for the fifth time, so they think you have had enough and will then come themselves. Men that want to bend you over and just bang away are few and far between, despite what most people think. Average guys still like you to be in charge, though, at the end, to please him back. Great work-out for the thighs, always being cowgirl on top, but bad on the knees after a while.

I took a day off on Sunday to sleep, eat and recuperate. It was wonderful, and better still knowing that my lock box was stuffed with newly earned money. That had been the last thing I had done before crashing out. The day before, I'd worked since noon and had come back just as late as I had from dancing, so it had been a long day, and even just sitting around trying to stay alert gets tiring. The sauna, so far, was so much better than working at the stripclub, but only time would tell if I could stick working every day like the rest of the girls did. I had only worked three days a week before, but here in London they required you to work at least five if you could. If I saw as many clients as I had the previous day, then it should be OK. It was only after ten in a shift that I preferred to take the next day off to recover. I probably could do a second day like that, but no more than that in a row. I would be far too swollen by then to be of much use other than to answer wanker phone calls. Layla reckoned she could do at least twelve and work the next day too, but she always was a show-off, and I told her so over the phone that afternoon when she called me and asked how it was going. She *is* nosey – but not as nosey as my family.

I was in a better mood after having had a chat to Layla, so I checked in with my mother next on the phone. She nattered happily away in my ear about news of home and things that had happened at family events, things she hadn't told me about, and then she realized she must have told my younger sister the same thing twice. It was nice to hear her, but an hour of your mother in your ear can make any sane person go a little deaf, especially if yours is deaf herself and tends to shout down the phone. My family aren't the quietest members of the human race; the next-door neighbours could tell anyone that.

I had called and heard my mother's normal response to me – 'So you're alive then?' – on the other end. I hadn't been down to see them in a while, blaming it on moving to London, so she had been bound to call and intrude at some point if I hadn't called her. If I didn't go down there soon, though, she might end up on my doorstep for a visit, and that would never do. Before I knew it, they would all be around, nosing in my business all the time and hard to get rid of, and then they might find out what I was really doing. (I had told them I was working as a night-security monitor for CCTV.) I couldn't see Claudia being at all happy if any of my family descended on us. She didn't like her peace and quiet to be spoiled; she already complained if I had the radio on in my room as I tidied my stuff, still in piles from moving, into bigger piles.

I only managed to escape deafness from the phone call with my mother by promising to go down and visit the following month, hoping she would forget all about it and that I could love my family from a distance and enjoy my own version of peace and quiet, left alone to do what I wished.

*

I'd been at the sauna some time now and, between having to pretty much barter with the clients over rates, which I found a bit degrading, and the fact there were only a few clients for all the girls, the so-called benefits of working in this brothel cum sauna weren't offset by my earning enough to save and become as flush financially as I'd hoped. Let's face it, living in London is never cheap, and even though I was now being paid more for each client, with the cost of living in the capital, I wasn't making or saving any more than I had in the past and, now, I was seeing from three to a maximum of seven clients a day, if I was lucky, so I was earning less than I had before. At least I was earning more than I had been at the stripclub, which was a start, I suppose.

To add to that, I was still feeling slightly unsettled where I was living. I hadn't warmed to Claudia at all, as I had to my previous flatmates; they had been my friends, and Claudia, quite plainly, was never going to be that. The flat didn't feel like home; in fact, it mostly made me feel on edge. The area was all red-brick council flats and it had me on my guard before I even got in the front door. In the past, if I hadn't liked something, I changed it, and it looked like this was one of these times. I needed to move, and probably very soon, since my hackles were up, and for no very good reason that I could see. Looking at it rationally, the rent was very cheap for central London.

I phoned my mum for a chat to see if it would change my mind and convince me to stay put, but it backfired completely. I had thought she would advise me against moving again, as I had just got to London and she could picture where I was in her mind's eye – 'nice and settled again', as she put it – but the damn woman completely floored me by saying she could hear I wasn't happy and maybe I should consider moving somewhere else in London, if it would make me happier. You think you know your mother, and then she ups and surprises you!

To my mother, who lived on the coast, it didn't matter where you were in London, it was all the same. Thank goodness she hadn't yet come up to visit – I could just imagine how worried she would be, going back home having seen the dark and foreboding council block I lived in and the sparse furniture in the flat, not to mention the fact that I was still sleeping on a mattress on the floor. After seeing that she would have called every day to check that I was all right and hadn't been mugged, burgled or murdered. And, to top it off, there would have been frequent visits from various members of the family to make sure that I was OK whenever they just happened to be 'passing by' London. That, I really didn't need. I had always been the sensible one in the family, the one Mum didn't need to worry about or bother, and I planned on keeping it that way.

I pottered off that day to the sauna with thoughts of moving out and where to go and asked the girls if any of them had a flat with a spare room or knew someone who was looking for a flatmate. No one had any ideas, but they all said they would ask around. I then spent the rest of what turned out to be a slow night looking in the papers for flats that were available to rent and within my budget. I would call them the next day.

After much ringing around, I realized that saying I was a dancer was not doing me any favours in selling myself as a tenant-to-be to landlords. It didn't sound too stable a position. One landlady grumbled but agreed to show me around what turned out to be a poky, rundown room on Baker Street. You couldn't swing a cat in it, it had a grubby shared toilet on the landing and she was asking twice the rent I was now paying. The hanging frayed electric-light fixture and the dodgy-looking cooker right next to the bed had me beating a hasty retreat – but I had a feeling most of the flats I would be shown would be similar.

A few days later, trying to reconcile myself to the fact that Claudia's flat wasn't that bad after all for the amount I was paying her, I ambled into work just as Emma was opening up the sauna. I helped her push up the black roller shutters that covered the blacked-out windows and black-plated door. She smiled cheerfully and told me that she had a friend who had a friend with a flat for rent in north London. It was just a bit more money than I had been looking to pay, but it was supposed to be a really nice new one-bedroom flat and was in a good area.

I thought about it all through my shift, sitting perched on her desk in my short massage uniform: it was a lot of money for me. By the time I had drunk the tea she had made and we had munched through half the packet of Hobnobs I had brought with me, I had realized that the new flat was double the rent I was now paying Claudia but, to be fair, cost around the same as most of the flats in central London. Emma prattled on and was just writing down the landlady's number when the buzzer buzzed.

The chap who walked in wanted to see Zora but she

was late in and he didn't have the time to wait. Seeing me, he said I would do. Gee, thanks, buster, I thought, leading him to the closest back room and leaving him there to have a shower. I was still pondering moving as I paid the room fee to Emma out of the £80 the man had given me. I left the £15 on the desk for her, as she was on the phone, and grabbed a towel from the cupboard as I passed.

I went through the motions, rubbing down the middle-aged accountant who was lying quite contentedly on the massage table before me. I asked him to turn over and I undid my uniform, slinging it over the rim of the bath where he had taken his shower, close behind me. My mind was still on the rent for the north London flat Emma had mentioned.

I had a rubber on him as soon as he turned over. I parked his cock in my mouth, sucking him fast to get him hard. *It did sound like a nice flat, and it even had a parking space.*

Percentage-wise, this guy wasn't getting any bigger. He groaned, putting his hand on the back of my head and trying to shove me further down his small semi-hard-on. Even though I knew from experience I was in danger of his choking me, I was not paying much attention. *Percentage-wise, it wasn't as if I was saving what I used to.*

I kicked off my shoes. *It was a big step moving out of central London now I was here and had found my feet.*

I peeled down my knickers, still giving him head and now removing my bra. He was trying to roughly grope one of my small tits with his free hand, which I didn't like. *Even though I didn't like my flatmate, it was still a lot of money to pay just so I didn't have to share.*

I climbed on top, tightened my internal muscles and sat down, very slowly, on his under-average cock. 'Mmm,' I mumbled. *Mmm, £150 a week, which is over double what I'm paying for where I'm staying at the moment and four times what I used to pay for rent ...*

I was now squatting on top of him, my feet either side, and I rose, squeezing his cock tighter as I pushed up with my feet. Ready to relax a bit, I slid down him again, already bracing to repeat the movement. *I had bought quite a few things now, including some bedroom furniture for my room. It would take a few trips up and down to north London to move. Ahhh, now, that might take a few days.*

'Ahhhhh,' I slurred, bouncing around on top of the balding man below me, rubbing my hands over his nipples to see if they were sensitive. *If I did move, at least I would have a flat all to myself, no vain flatmate. If it was as nice as it sounded, my mother, if she did visit, wouldn't feel the need to bother me much or worry afterwards.*

The man drew a breath below me as his nipples hardened at my touch. *I could decorate and sleep when I wanted to – even fall asleep on the sofa and not be bothered by anyone and, more importantly, do what I wanted when I wanted to ... Oooh, now that was a thought.*

I let out the 'Oooh' as I pinched his nipples. He made a face, shook beneath me and came on time. *Maybe it was about time I did move, after all.*

I climbed off and asked the man if he was OK. I then grabbed a tissue to take off the condom, as I always did, from the box on the windowsill, just to make sure there was no split in the rubber, to check it over. *Right – all I had to do was make contact, check it over.*

I tidied myself up and put my robe back on as the man dressed in a hurry, even more so when he noted the time, which had flown by. I showed him out and he dashed for a cab to catch a morning meeting he was already late for. Emma smiled at me as I turned to close the door behind him. She was waving the phone number she had scribbled down for me earlier.

It was the weekend and I was having lunch in the flat, my sandwich perched precariously on my lap, for want of a better place in our tableless lounge. Claudia was not around, as normal, not surprising, as her lunchtime trysts with (from what I could work out) her sugar daddy always spread into late afternoon. Her sugar daddy was twice her age, if not more, and was supposedly paying her half of the rent, though he thought he was paying for the whole flat for her alone. He was the reason I wasn't allowed to pick up the phone if it rang, or answer the door, which was a moot point as, for some reason, he never came round anyhow. Claudia said that she just had lunch with him and that there was nothing sexual about their relationship – but no girl gets that many shoes as gifts without at least putting out from time to time. She would get really prissy about it all though, so I could never be bothered to bring it up.

Anyhow, lunch was interrupted when a short guy and two larger guys walked in the front door. The short guy was the owner of the flat, and he asked what I was doing there. I said I paid Claudia rent to live there.

The owner said Ali, Claudia's ex-, was his little brother and he had been supposed to look after the flat, rent one of the rooms out and, with that money, pay the bills and do the flat up for his, the brother's, return from working abroad. The landlord had come back the week before to England, rung on the phone a few times and got no answer. Neither me nor Claudia ever picked up the phone. He didn't know that his brother had moved out, and that the flat had been sublet again. The bills hadn't been paid, so he had assumed it was empty. He hadn't been able to get hold of his brother, who had mysteriously disappeared on holiday for a few weeks, so here he was, and he had brought some guys around with him who wanted the flat. They had already agreed between themselves that they could rent the flat and move in the following week.

He didn't look best pleased that his wishes hadn't been carried out and got straight on to the phone to his little brother, who didn't or wouldn't pick up. All dues to the man, he wasn't taking it out on me; if I had been in the same position, I don't know how calm I would have remained, coming into my property to find a drawerful of letter threats from the council over unpaid tax and, to top it off, what looked like squatters, when he thought the flat was empty.

The new tenants looked around and then left. The landlord and I worked out between us that Claudia had been giving his brother, Ali, half the rent and keeping my half. Ali had been pocketing it and not paying the bills either, not that he'd known about them, as Claudia had been putting them, unopened, in a kitchen drawer, thinking they didn't matter. My take on Claudia as an elusive, greedy, money-grabbing bitch hadn't been as far off the mark as it might have seemed. What is it with people!

The landlord sympathized and said it wasn't my fault but, even so, I would have to move out soon. He would look out for another flat for me if I wanted, which I thanked him for, but he said he wasn't going to help Claudia; he didn't trust her. That made two of us then.

We exchanged numbers, but he never did call and, after a few attempts and left messages to see if he knew of somewhere to rent, I gave up.

I told Claudia what had happened when she came back a couple of hours later. She was fuming and tried to call her ex-. No luck: he had turned off his phone. Then, in a sulk, she called her sugar daddy for help finding a new flat.

I asked her casually how much he gave her for the rent, or as casually as you can to a sulking, pissed-off Russian, and she said she had told him it was double what it was so she got to keep half, as he never gave her money for lunch.

I kept my mouth shut about the unpaid bills and worked out that in fact I was paying the rent and she was pocketing the sugar daddy's money and living in the flat for free, lying to me all the while. She was in such a state – worried about being kicked out – I don't think she realized what she was telling me.

I already had a plan but I hadn't yet called the number Emma had given me for the expensive flat in Muswell Hill. It was time to bite the bullet. I had had no luck with the abysmal central London offerings, so I left a message on the number as soon as I could. I wasn't in as much of a panic as I could have been – at least it looked like

71

I might have somewhere to go rather than being kicked out on to the street.

Where I was now, I was having to pay an astronomical rate for parking. There were no parking spots outside the red-brick block, which was a pain as parking meters in central London just eat money, and even using the option of parking lots a bit out of the centre was expensive. Even if you use the cheaper ones, like those around King's Cross, the costs add up and, with my rent and other outgoings, it was a big drain on my finances. I had to be paying at least £50 a week in parking fees to live in central London, money I'd save living in the smart, modern flat in Muswell Hill with its free parking spot. The money would all even out, and I would no longer be paying to have the sponging Claudia live off me. It was further out of the centre, but I would have a one-bedroom flat all to myself.

As soon as I had the chance, I went up and looked around the north London flat, even though the landlady owner was still living there. I said I would take it but I would have to move in three days' time, on Sunday, as I had to be out of my flat by then. I was thinking I might need to stay in a hotel for a while, but she said that Sunday would be fine; that they – her boyfriend and her – were half moved anyway, into his place, which was a great relief to me.

The flat was at the end of a posh, quiet road of cottages. Inside, it was cosy, with a big floor-to-ceiling window that gave on to a great view of trees in the park below. It was a new housing-association block, and the landlady's one stipulation was that I couldn't open the door to just anyone, because it might be the association checking up and, officially, she wasn't allowed to sublet. That was fine by me. I didn't even answer the door to the postman, let alone to unscheduled and unannounced callers. I was way too paranoid for that.

No one just popped in to see me now that I had moved away. Even good friends like Layla and Sanita, my ex-flatmates and still working girls themselves down south, knew to call before coming around, especially as they knew I had been stalked the year before, and it wasn't like I had made many friends now I had moved to London. The landlady's stipulation gave me a great excuse to tell my family there was no way they could pop around unannounced or without letting me know well in advance. My new landlady didn't need references; she said as her friend knew Emma, the receptionist, she knew where I worked and she had no problem with it, saying that at least she knew I earned well and could pay her, and that was good enough for her. She had met Emma, who, unbeknown to me, had vouched for me, saying in passing that I was a good little earner and no hassle, which I suppose had strengthened my case.

The landlady called me the next day and said they had cleared the lounge already and I could bring stuff around and leave it there if I liked. I liked her. She was pretty easygoing.

I took the next couple of days off work to pack and move, and did ten car trips with my stuff. Claudia was still panicking that her sugar daddy hadn't found her a place to move to yet, and we had to be out by Sunday. Initially, she didn't even ask where I was going. I mentioned it in passing, while taking bin bags of my clothes and stuff out to the car. 'North London' was all I said, when she eventually asked on one of my last trips out to the car. She turned up her nose and said, 'Far too far from shops. I won't move there,' prancing off with her latest copy of *Vogue*. I hadn't asked her opinion, cheeky cow.

Early Sunday morning I left the door key on the kitchen sideboard of the red-brick council flat with a good-luck note to Claudia and drove to the new flat without a backwards glance. I was off to live and settle by myself in a really nice place in leafy north London.

6. *Mr Body*

I had been at the sauna for quite a few months, and the going was still slow. If five men a day came in during the week it was considered busy. It picked up a bit at the weekend, but it wasn't as busy as it had been. I was working at least five days a week, if not more, and it was all getting dull, just going through the motions.

I was in early, as usual, and was waiting for the other girls to arrive.

'Morning, honey. Looks like we have some new girls.'

Zora blustered in past me. I started filing a broken nail and got up to peep over the saloon doors that separated the girls seated in the corner corridor and the entrance reception room. Sitting there were two smartly dressed, dark-haired girls, chatting to the receptionist and clutching their handbags to their expensively suited laps.

I turned around and followed Zora down to the dark basement room where she was heading. 'Who are they? Social workers? Journos?' I asked her.

They looked too sharp and smelled too expensive to be sauna working girls. I had spotted their smart handbags and shoes, and one of them even had a designer watch glinting on her wrist.

'Escorts sniffing around,' she mumbled, heaving her bag after her and continuing down the stairs to change out of her scruffy jeans and into her white uniform.

'Escorts? I thought they were called call girls?' I was still following her, clipping down the steep steps in my heels.

'Nah, that's Americans on TV. Over here they are called escorts, for some reason. Something to do with paying for their time and not what they do – you know, escorting a punter to functions and stuff,' she muttered, rummaging through her bag in the middle of the floor.

'OK. So what do escorts in London do then?' I leaned against the wall and flipped on another light switch so she could see to find what she was searching for.

'Exactly the same as us; they just have more time to do it and they normally go to the punter on outcalls, so it's more risky. That's why they get paid more.' She fished out her hairbrush and set about her hair with one hand, picking out her shoes with the other. She was late and really in a rush, although I couldn't see why, as there were no clients in to say hello to. It was way too early for that. It wasn't like there was ever a lunchtime rush.

'I'll leave you to it and go and listen in upstairs then,' I said, turning to go back up to see what was happening in reception.

I had heard about outcalls to clients' houses from Layla. No one had called the girls anything as glam as escorts at the time, she said. She had told me all about it the year before, when I had worked with her at the brothel. When she started there, the house had been offering outcalls to men in the local area at £55, which was £15 more than the house rate at the brothel. She had done two outcalls, and they had been OK, but it had taken her a lot longer to get there and back than she had thought it would and Mrs Boss hadn't been too happy. Mrs Boss thought Layla was missing out on bookings during the time it took to travel to the outcall, and the money you got didn't compensate for the time. They had only had three girls working then and were getting busier, as it was a new brothel and the news was spreading.

It wasn't till the third outcall booking, when Layla had been sent to an estate at the top of a hill, that there was a problem. The client, unbeknown to her or the brothel, had locked her in. Outcalls being all new to her, she didn't notice until she was on her knees giving the chap a blow job in his lounge, when she heard a rattle and a bang on the front, locked door and a woman screeching through the letterbox. His wife was shouting how she was going to kill the bitch he had with him and that she had seen what he was up to through the window.

Layla said she was then thankful he had locked the door, but that wasn't the point: she was locked in, and now she couldn't leave, as the bloke's wife was outside, going berserk, thinking he had a mistress on the side. In the end Mr Boss had to go and rescue her out through the back door of the client's house while the bloke opened the front door to the screaming woman and confronted her. I asked her what had happened next, and she said the bloke had called from A&E to see if she had got home safely, as he was nursing a bump on his head and a black eye after being thrown out by his wife. After that, the brothel had decided that it was too dangerous to send its girls on outcalls and that they could make more money by seeing an extra client in the time it took to travel to and fro, so they didn't see the point in all the extra hassle. This story was why I accepted what had been said about girls who didn't work in a house – in my mind, it wasn't safe doing outcall stuff. If Layla, of all people, didn't do it, then it must be on a par with the dangers I imagined girls working on the street would face.

I had never met an agency escort until Sonya, the Slovakian (so she said), and her tall skinny friend had walked into the sauna I was now working at. They had come into reception after ringing for an interview as they had heard you could make money faster in a sauna than in an agency. Sonya said to me that afternoon that she hadn't thought it would be as quiet or as low-paid working here at the sauna as it was. Her friend didn't speak much English, so they huddled in the corner whispering away as I finished painting a snagged nail.

My mind was racing. Why make the switch from an agency to a sauna rather than just going to a different agency? And, if they were complaining at the low rates we charged, and the fact that you had to pretty much barter with the clients (the bit I hated), how much did *they* get paid?

Sonya was going back to her agency in the morning, as it wasn't busy enough for her here, and her friend was going with her. As she was leaving, she leaned in close to me in the corridor. 'Why do you work here? You are not old like the others. Wouldn't you earn more as an escort?' She looked me up and down, a confused expression on her face. 'You would do well.' She patted my arm gently in a friendly way.

I said to her that I didn't know much about it, and

I wouldn't know where to start finding out. It was then I asked, 'Isn't it very dangerous? You hear all the chatter about girls being locked in, gang raped or stuffed in the boots of cars, don't you?' All the horror stories I had heard from the other girls and the madam had stayed in my mind.

'Where did you hear that? Itz not like that at all ... maybe at the cheaper end, but we don't have to works for them, those pimpz.' She virtually spat. 'They take care of you in the good agency.' She was nodding away as she spoke.

'But the newspapers and the girls and the owner here talk about all the bad stuff that goes on. That's why I work here – it's safer,' I carried on. I was still unsure about her. Call me Miss Paranoid, but if everything was great there, why was she looking for work here?

She raised her eyebrow at me. 'Yezz, I think the owner 'ere would say itz bad to be escort, to keeps you 'ere.' She did have a point.

She was busy rummaging in her old Louis Vuitton bag and brought out a bent red card, which she popped down my top before I could take it from her manicured talons.

''Ere, this is where I normally work, a sit-in escort agency. The owner, she is a lush, but itz better than most.'

She winked and dashed off, grabbing her coat and her friend as she went. With that, they cut their losses and left without poor Emma on reception being able to stop them or ask where they were going.

I waited till I was downstairs in the basement before I pulled the crumpled card out of my non-existent cleavage and had a look at it. Written on it in black was the name of the agency, an address and phone number. I put it in the side pocket of my bag and, hearing the door buzz, ran upstairs to say hello. Fingers crossed this one was mine, and then, maybe, it would soon be time to leave and shut up the knocking shop.

The day was bright and I had earned well in the days after my encounter with the escort. My conversation with her was still fresh in my mind. Who knew – maybe you did earn a bit more escorting, but did I really want to take the risk? Probably not. Mind you, having said that, the previous evening hadn't been all plain sailing in the sauna. It hadn't been a day that the madam normally drifted in and, when she did, the girls had to scatter to tidy up and grab their laundry out of the non-used sauna. She had swanned in looking like she had all the time in the world to hang around and chat. There were at least five of us on shift that day and it was a packed house, so she had a full audience. There didn't seem to be much consistency in the rota at the sauna; it looked like any girl who wanted to work could work a shift whenever she wanted. We were supposed to work at least five a week, but it was all very erratic. They didn't have very many girls as it was, so the madam didn't have much choice. Only four of us were fairly permanent, and then there were the odd few girls who started and then disappeared after a shift or two. Today was obviously a popular day to work.

After a ruckus with a late-night drunk the previous evening the boss had come in to check on Emma, who was still more than a little rattled, and to thank Ebony for her help with removing the drunk.

Thank goodness Ebony worked the night shifts was all I could think: she was the only girl big enough, at a hefty six foot, to possibly stand up to or remove a guy from the premises. She didn't get as much work as the other girls, but I was sure the other week she had only given over £5 for her room fee to Emma rather than the obligatory £15 and then had dashed off to tend to her client while Emma put it away in the drawer without making any fuss. I thought it was odd at the time, but now I was wondering if Ebony had an agreed reduced room rate to pay as recompense for being a helping hand. Receptionists were normally burly enough and old enough, with a very sharp tongue to deal with any problems. It was only then it dawned on me that, with Ebony in her corner, the young, petite receptionist had all the help she needed.

Our madam was leaning on the frame of the saloon door and was relating a tale she had heard just recently about a dreadful beating some poor escort had received at the hands of a pimp, much to the shock of a new girl in the corner, especially as the girls then started to speculate about other nasty things they had heard of. I looked up at our boss lady, who was looking rather too pleased with herself at all the horror stories being bandied about, and I couldn't help wondering what had tickled her fancy. The other girls were all too deep in their gossip by then to notice, all talking about how dangerous it was to work as an unprotected escort and how nice and safe we were working here. Looking at the grin on the madam's face, I heard Sonya the Slovakian's voice in my head, saying the other day that of course the boss would bring up things like this to keep us working for her. My previous Mrs Boss had said very similar things about the dangers of working for places in London, that they were all run by pimps who would beat their girls, and that street girls got raped and robbed. She never had much of a good word for strippers either. The brothel had made out that working for a sauna in London was dire, a last resort, and the sauna here in London was doing the same, but giving the impression that it was even worse to work for a brothel, not just in the bad ones in London (which I had a feeling was actually true) but all over England. I was beginning to think that Sonya might be right. Hell, if I was a boss I might stir up the same sort of thing if it meant keeping my girls working for me. It may be sneaky but it was effective.

The stories continued even after the madam had left, but they did start to subside as the afternoon wore on. As there was a lack of seats in the lounge with so many girls on shift, I sat in the reception and chatted to Emma, who wasn't quite her normal bubbly self. While I was talking to her the thought started to niggle at me that she was more one of us than a receptionist. From what I could work out from having talked to her before, she had worked in a sauna some time back but was now happy enough working the desk, even if the money wasn't as good as she used to get. After a while, I left to find Zora, who was sitting in the sauna drying the stockings she had just washed, now that the madam had left.

'OK, I give up.' I kicked off my heels as I opened the smoked-glass door to the four-person sauna. I had been there the day before when the loud drunk had stumbled in, plonked himself on Emma's desk and demanded she suck his cock for a fiver – or something of the sort. I was downstairs when it all kicked off – it had been a slow night and I was watching the clock, getting ready to leave – so I hadn't seen how Emma handled the situation. I heard the shouting in reception from the basement and bounded up the stairs in bare feet, just in time to catch Ebony launching the drunk out of the door with a forceful push. While it was still going on, Emma could have called the police, but they wouldn't have been there in time. The drunk had lost it and was starting to lash out and spit, and when she asked him to leave he had lain on her desk and hung on. That was the situation Ebony had found when she went to help get him out and in the process rescue Emma.

Zora looked up, hanging her last stocking over a towel rail in the wooden box, as I came in and the dry heat hit me. She raised her eyebrows, and I went on. 'You've been here the longest, right? What's the score with Emma? Come on, spill: why is she on the desk?'

Zora pursed her lips and laid back against a towel. I pulled one from the small stack between us and put it down so I wouldn't have to sit on the wooden slats.

'Why? What have you heard, Shell?' Zora stretched her legs out on the bench and leaned towards me. She sounded suspicious.

I shrugged. 'Nothing really. It's just that, between you and me, I don't get it. Why did the boss lady hire her?'

Zora leaned back. 'Ahh, that's between you and me.' She looked over at the glass door and I shuffled closer. Zora was always a mine of information. 'Emma used to work for the madam's son in his Camden sauna last year. She did really well, was one of their top girls. They really liked her.' She looked over through the door again.

'I just bet they did,' I muttered. I could imagine how well a bubbly, pretty blonde like Emma would do in one of the biggest, most popular, cheap saunas in the area. She would probably have been so busy there was no need for her to wear her knickers. Well-proportioned, she was the typical wet wank dream.

'There was an incident with one of the clients. It was a busy night and she was in one of the back rooms which they hardly ever used. The fucking room-security buzzer didn't work; she dived for it and rang it but no one came to help her. The boss had popped out for beer and left another girl in charge, and the dopey girl didn't know that Emma was on shift. The bloke raped Emma, un-protected, at knife point for over an hour, and tied her to the table and gagged her so he could leave without any fuss. The boss came back and found her a couple of hours after that. They never caught the guy and Emma didn't want to report it to the coppers. If she had the son would have had hell to pay, all the heat from the police nosing in. And, of course, his dad's in the slammer, owns the property. They really don't need the coppers sniffing around there.' I shifted in the heat as I started to sweat and fanned myself with a magazine that had been left. I guessed they had made Emma a receptionist here out of gratitude as, from what Zora had said, I doubt Emma would want to be in a room alone with any man any time soon. I was surprised she still had the bottle to work in a sauna at all.

'Guess that's why Emma didn't deal very well with the drunk last night. She's still a bit shaky today.'

Zora nodded. 'Yeah, Shell. She'll be OK though, she's a tough little cookie. Pity she didn't have a safety buddy like I have with Ebony, she could have done with one.' I nodded back. A lot of things were beginning to make sense.

I knew Ebony and Zora came into work together. I had bumped into them as Zora's hubby was dropping them both off that morning. I hadn't realized up to then that neither worked without the other – it just hadn't dawned on me – but thinking back on it, I had never seen one here when the other wasn't. I didn't like to press Zora any further, as I had only found out that morning that she had a husband who not only knew and had no problem with where she worked and what she did but dropped her off at work too, by the look of it. Apparently, it was fine; they swang. I must have looked even more confused than usual. I had the image of some kind of fetish swing contraption in my head and was trying to work out why that would mean that Zora's hubby, a smiling, well-built Aussie, didn't mind his missus shagging men for money. Ebony had shaken her head at my mystified 'Swings?' question and said, 'They're swingers, silly.' Zora had been there and coughed a full-bellied laugh while Ebony chortled.

I left Zora in the sauna as Ebony came in to join her and went off to make a cup of tea, popping my nose round the corner to ask if Emma wanted one, too, rattling my Hobnobs at her. 'Nob?' was out of my mouth before I had a chance to think about it. Luckily, she giggled and said, 'Yes, please.'

*

So now I was settled, earning fairly well, my mother had come up to visit for the weekend and she was very happy that I was happy, and in a nice part of London, so she would leave me well alone, much to my relief. I was still keeping to my night-work story to explain the odd hours I was sleeping and why I looked so pale. After she had left I was on the rota at the sauna nearly every day but, despite all the clients I was seeing, I did notice I was getting a bit hornier than usual. OK, so the men who had come in the past week had all been average massage screws, a few blow-job guys thrown in for good measure; none of them had pressed any buttons for me and, with my vibrator running out of batteries the night before and the ones in the TV remote in my lounge the wrong type to help that morning, I was wound tighter than a spring and had to stop myself driving twice around a round-about on my way into work to perve on a really well-built policeman.

That was probably one of the reasons I took a shine to one of my clients that evening. It was unusual for me to do that. I always liked to keep work separate from free sex. I had seen what happened countless times when girls started to date their regular clients. It always got messy and the girls would get into a state and it would disrupt their earning potential. Anyhow, that evening, a short black bodybuilder, Mr Body, had been dragged in by his mate, whose birthday it was. The so-called mate was white, six foot four, if not taller, with blue eyes and spiky blond hair. He was also drunk or stoned – I couldn't tell which – and looked a bit of a handful. I instantly pre-ferred the quieter, sober black guy. I had had bad shags all that day and I was not really in the mood to deal with another: no matter how much he looked like a Greek god, because he was tipsy I was betting he would have one hell of a yo-yo cock. Unfortunately, the birthday boy was leering at me. Damn, and with only me and the small Chinese girl, who, appropriately, named herself Suk-suk, one of us was bound to get him and, as it was his birthday, or so he said, I was just guessing he would get to pick first. Double damn, especially as Suk-suk was going all giggly over the blond.

We made our introductions and retreated to the lounge benches for them to make up their minds. The silly girl could have him. I got called through first, dragging my feet as I heard the black guy loudly hiss at the birthday boy as he rose from the leather couch they had both sunk into that he didn't want to see some 'Chink'. He looked me up and down with a dark glint in his eye like he had only just really seen me. At my bemused look he strode over and gestured me to show him the way.

Mumbling this and that, we wound ourselves up the slim, tight spiral staircase to find a room on the upper floor. I didn't think the tipsy birthday boy could man-age the stairs and so Suk-suk could have the bigger ground-floor room. She would need it, and it was closer if she needed Emma's help. I didn't think I would need any. Following up behind Mr Body on the stairs, I was very nearly drooling, looking at the way his tight trousers hugged his bum. Very nice.

I showed him to a room and said I would leave him to have a shower, as I did all the men. I looked him over as he started to unbutton his shirt. I turned to leave – it didn't mean I couldn't pop back more quickly than normal and catch him in the shower though. He tried to stop me, saying he had just had a shower. I was in no mood for silly games and said, 'Please, out of consideration for my health,' turning to leave before he could get a word in, saying I needed to get more towels. With him being so broad I didn't think one towel was going to be enough to dry him. 'When you're done, just pop up on the bench face down for the massage and I'll be back in to rub you down,' I rambled on, retreating out of the door and shutting it on my last word. I had worked out early on that if I didn't give the clients the chance to speak, then they wouldn't have the opportunity to say no to pretty much anything I asked. It's easier to handle a near-naked man when you're still fully dressed. This one seemed OK, but he was wound tight and a bit stressed, so if I took charge now, he wouldn't be able to give me any bullshit.

I waited outside until I heard the shower running and then left him to it. If a guy was going to be a hassle even when you asked him to take a shower, or refused outright, you knew he was going to be trouble the whole way through. But making a guy get naked while you still had your clothes on put you automatically in control and made him more vulnerable and less likely to try it on and mess you around. To be honest, most guys were fairly clean, and asking them to shower didn't necessarily mean they would wash properly in any case. And I would always have a shower afterwards anyhow, so it didn't really matter much. Asking Mr Body to shower was more about control and, considering his size, I really needed to be more than in control. I like a man to be where I want him, in the palm of my hand, and when they're naked it's so much easier.

I had a feeling he was very nervous. I guessed it hadn't been his idea to come in and play. His friend had already given Emma £200, and she had told us it was to be split between Suk-suk and I before we went in to introduce ourselves to them. By the time I had left my guy in the shower and nipped down the stairs to grab two towels, Suk-suk was leading the blond guy into the downstairs room and looking very pleased with herself. I checked in with Emma and told her to keep hold of my money, minus the room cut, until after I was done, just so I didn't have to worry about it. I rushed back up the stairs to try and catch my guy dripping wet in the shower. The artist in me had already seen that he worked out a lot; he had a very impressive physique. I walked back in without even knocking to see a damp, glistening back stretched out, a towel around the hips.

I had been right, but he was more than just fit, he had muscles on his muscles. No wonder he had looked as if he was tense. I chatted away with him and put all my attention into unknotting the tension in his large back, undoing my uniform as I went. No trouble, no hassle, and with his dry sense of humour, which I could appreciate, we were getting on like a house on fire before I even had him turned over. I stood back and unpeeled very slowly, tossing him my bra as he sat up and unclipping the side fastenings of my knickers as I walked back to him. Upright now, his legs were dangling over the massage table and there was a big grin on his face. I approached and stroked his cock with my right hand, the one I normally use to touch men with.

Drawing my fingers down his length, I looked him in the eye as I tightened my grip. I hadn't expected him to be as huge there as the rest of him was; I had done enough research on the human body to know that bodybuilders' bulk tended to overshadow things in that department. Mr Body wasn't small, but he wasn't a python either. He had promising girth but a fairly average-length cock. I was more than happy with him though and, considering how horny I was feeling, it suited me not having to do yet another boring grey accountant type in a suit. Stroking his cock as he flicked my nipples, I pushed him further back from the edge with a hand on his large chest as I reached for the rubber in my stocking top and sucked it on him. He grunted and leaned back, braced on his elbows, as I sucked him and ran my fingers over his cleanly shaven balls, making him harder.

I kicked off my shoes, withdrawing to climb up on to the seat next to the table. Without the chair it was way too high to get up there. I crawled across the end to where he was propped and knelt up, ready to swing my leg over his lap and slide down his hard length, but just as I was about to do so, he caught my pussy between his fingers and flicked my clit. Before I realized why, I had gasped, and he moved his lips on to the breast closest to him with a wicked grin. His fingers lightly probed, sliding in my lubed-up lips, and fondled as he worked on, licking my nipple. I shuddered at the progress his naughty fingers were making and let him slide one digit up, grasping it with my internal muscles just to let him know how tight I was going to make it for him.

At that, he jerked his head up. For some reason it had startled him. The light grin on his face had all but gone now, replaced with a dark look I could only guess the meaning of. I wriggled on his finger, snug inside, then he withdrew and I took advantage quickly and sat over his lap, hovering over his firm cock with my knees pushed apart, either side of his steel-hard thighs. He gripped my buttocks as I slithered down, tilting my hips to accommodate him easily, until I was in place, ready to tighten up and slide down him. That was all it took for him to buck and lift me into slow thrusts, with his arms under me pulling me in tightly every time.

I let go of the edge, literally as well as physically, which wasn't the best thing to do a couple of feet off the floor on a now wobbly bench, as I nearly toppled off. For such a bulky guy, he managed to swing me under him and carry on his pounding as I wrapped not only my legs around him but my cunt too. He felt so smooth all over and, in the darkened room, with him blocking out the light, my mind was all over the place as I came and came hard. Losing control was not something that was a good idea while at work, but from the feel of it he was losing it too, which made me feel a lot better.

He was rolling around and I was on top. How we managed it without falling off must have been down to his strength as, with my legs wound securely around him, he managed to lift me with him, and around him with one arm, so that as he rolled over I slid my legs from under him and secured them at his sides, squatting over him, cowgirl-style. Sitting on top, my best position to make a man come, I rode him, rocking back and forth and trying to make it last but realizing that time was running out. I made a faster stroke, and he looked like he had been shot when I felt him come. I stretched and slowly wriggled, pulsing my pussy around his hot cock as he gulped deep breaths to steady himself as he came back down. His heart was pounding still. I could feel it in his chest as I lay my hands over the tight, smooth surface. I had needed that, and it took me a few seconds before I could get my own breath back to ease off him and find the tissues.

I hadn't been that breathless in quite some time. I had definitely needed the work-out, I told him, as I tidied up and ran the shower for him. He patted my bottom, and I would have joined him in there but didn't trust my or his hands not to wander and, as time was very nearly up, I was aware that his friend was probably downstairs waiting for him. I quickly got dressed and rubbed him down when he got out of the shower – any excuse to rub a naked man down, I know – but this naked man felt really nice under my fingers. We chatted and flirted as he dressed. He was definitely keen, and said that he worked security on the door of a club and that if any of the girls and I wanted to go clubbing to let him know and he would get us in for free. Nice of him, but I doubted I wanted to let any of the other girls know I might be copping off with a punter, not that he was really a punter.

He said he wouldn't be back, as it was only his mate who liked to come to saunas. I knew for certain he hadn't come in voluntarily. The birthday boy was on 'too many of the wrong steroids,' or so Mr Body said, and having seen the six-foot-plus bulging blond earlier, with his bugged-out eyes, I could fully believe it. His mate had been going on and on all week about coming here, getting on his nerves, so he had finally agreed to a boys' night out. I was grinning from ear to ear as he smirked, saying he was glad he had come – very glad. I'd had a really bad week and he, with his magic fingers, had really cheered me up and, as a bonus, all I'd had to do was sit on his dick – and he had done most of the work! There had been no stopping the man, he was like a jack hammer. I was very impressed. I couldn't help wondering: he had already made me come – with a proper bed and more time, imagine what an orgasm he would give me.

He couldn't give me his personal number, as we didn't have a pen and I couldn't go down looking for one, as time had run out and it would have looked very suss. He gave me one of the cards of the nightclub he worked for and told me to ask for Tony on the front door; that was him. They would call him to the phone and we could swap numbers, if I was up for it? After that performance I didn't want to sound too eager, so I nodded maybe and slid the card into my stocking top as we left the room to find his friend. With me looking around for a better place, I didn't think keeping his number would do any harm as long as I rang it after I stopped working there.

I thought he was single – after all, he didn't mention a wife or wear a ring – but you never really know. He looked as if he would be more than happy if I needed to call him up when I was horny, and it wasn't like he had actually given me any money: his friend had; he hadn't actually placed money in my hand like the others did. In my mind, it was as if he hadn't actually paid me, as if he wasn't really a punter. Mmmm, my own personal sex toy, batteries not included. Hell – they weren't even needed!

7. *Girlfriend Experience*

Layla came to stay during her Christmas break from university. She was still living down south with Sanita and a few others in a big five-bedroom student house. Sanita had gone back to stay with her family up north till uni started again, which we found a bit strange, as she normally avoided them like the plague. She had left the brothel and was no longer hooking, Layla told me with a shrug. It hadn't been long, but it was nice to see Layla again and have her stay and keep me company for a while. The sofa was big enough to sleep on and she was very content to camp in my lounge and mooch around Muswell Hill for a few weeks. She was thinking of going back down south to continue working at the brothel but implied that it was going downhill fast and got me to spill the facts, as far as I knew them, about saunas, or 'fancy brothels', as she called them, here in London. After a chat about my chance meeting with Sonya, the escort I had met, and having shown Layla the card I had been given, her eyes lit up. She said we should at least give it a go but that it would be a good idea maybe to take a look at a few – after all, a girl who had to go and check out work in a sauna as she wasn't earning enough wasn't much of a recommendation for her agency. Added to that, we were very cautious, given Layla's past bad experience, and all the negative things I had heard about escorting.

Looking through the central London papers, we found a couple of likely agencies, and Layla called a few to enquire. One slammed the phone down on her when all she had said was hello. Two didn't pick up. One was really rude and said, no, they didn't need any more girls and then put the phone down. Two, including the one that Sonya had recommended, gave us details and dates for an interview. After a few calls Layla was really eager to go and check them out.

Three days later, at 2.50 p.m., Layla and I were sitting in my car looking over at the office-like front of the building across the road.

We had dressed in suits, with smart shoes, just as if we were going to an office interview. We hadn't been sure what to expect, and that's what the raspy lady on the phone had said to wear.

Layla, with me in tow, pressed the doorbell, which was underneath a little brass plaque on which was written 'International Ltd', at 3 p.m. precisely. It buzzed open abruptly to reveal a bespectacled, bronzed Mediterranean lady in her late forties with a bouffant hairstyle dyed jet-black, and dressed all in black, seated at the desk on our immediate left. I walked in, Layla hanging back.

'Hello. We called yesterday?' I said as I reached over the desk to shake her outstretched hand.

'Yes.' She nodded, and a strong smell of whisky wafted over to us.

'Take a seat.' She gestured to the low Chesterfield couch against the wall on the right behind me. Layla nodded as she closed the door behind her, and we both went to sit on the sofa.

'Can you start this week, either of you?' mumbled the woman behind the desk, rummaging in her desk. We nodded, a bit bemused, because we hadn't even started talking yet.

'Right. You will both have to fill out a form so I can remember who you are, and you will have to sign a contract on the day you start. It's just in case the law gets nosey, it doesn't mean anything really.

'Have you escorted before?' she asked, handing two forms and a pen over the desk to Layla.

'Sort of – we worked in saunas,' said Layla, taking the forms out of the dark-tanned, wrinkly hands festooned with gold rings.

Ms Lush slowly sank back into her chair. 'So, where did you hear of us?'

I took a form from Layla and looked up. 'A girl from one of the saunas I worked at in south London mentioned she had worked here.'

'Who?' Ms Lush leaned closer to us, a puckered, frowning look on her face.

'She was calling herself Sonya?' I raised my eyebrows, hoping Sonya hadn't fallen out of favour.

'Ahh, yessss.' She smiled and put her hand out. 'Give the forms here; I'll fill them out. I only have one pen and we don't have all day – the rest of the girls will be in soon.' Her blood-red talons took back the forms and the pen. 'What are your working names? Real names will just confuse me.' She gestured at Layla, her pen now reinstated in her clutch.

'Layla.'

Ms Lush nodded slowly. 'OK. We had a Layla, but she's left. She was like you – busty, too, and popular – so we can send you out as her if we're asked. They won't know the difference.' Layla just gave me one of her looks as Ms Lush bent over the form she was filling in.

Our interviewer then pointed at me, the pen still clasped in her hand.

'Scarlet?' I shrugged.

She nodded. 'That's OK. We haven't had one of them yet. Goes with the hair, but we might have to change it.' She noted something on the other form.

'Er, my name will have to change?' I was baffled.

Out of the corner of my eye, I could see that Layla was also looking baffled.

'No' – Ms Lush looked me in the eye – 'the hair, your hair. If you were blonde you would do better. Ginger is offputting, guys don't ask for ginger.' With that she swiftly moved on to the next question. I nodded, still a bit confused as to whether I was Scarlet or now called Ginger.

'Now, do you do O level?'

'Errr, well, I have a few GCSEs and a – ' I was quickly interrupted by a huffing noise.

'Nooo. Guys don't really care about your education, not really. What I mean is, do you do oral? It's called O levels, you know, it's code ... so I don't have to say anything about our services down the line.' Again, she leaned closer to us over the desk, and breathed in a whisper, 'You never know who's listening!' She stared at us with raised eyebrows and straightened up. 'Well, do you?'

'Oral on the client, yes,' Layla piped up. I looked at Layla, and the two of us nodded away, both thinking by this point that the woman was nutty as a fruitcake. What was with everything being in code? I thought we working girls were the paranoid ones!

'What about A levels?' Ms Lush peered over her big glasses at us. 'Anal,' she said bluntly.

We must have both looked horrified, because she mumbled, 'I'll take that as a no then. Girlfriend experience?' She looked up at us questioningly.

I looked at Layla who said, 'Uhh, duos?' She looked from me to Ms Lush as she said it, confused, the same as I was.

Ms Lush shook her head, looked back down at her form and huffed, 'Do you kiss?'

She looked up to see two puzzled-looking girls shaking their heads and sinking into the leather couch. 'No?' She huffed again, reached for a cigarette packet on the desk and tapped one out. 'That's OK, they don't really ask for that, if they want that they can get it from the wife ...' She muttered away as she lit the fag now hanging from her lips. 'So that's pornstar experience out then ...'

I mouthed, 'Pornstar experience?' and looked questioningly at Layla. She shrugged and shook her head. We decided it was better not to ask.

'OK. Contact numbers?' The lush looked up, scattering ash from her fag into her lap as she did so.

With that we gave her our mobile-phone numbers and asked about hours of work. She mentioned more than once that the agency was sit-in only and no in-call business; either our clients would come in to pick us and take us out to their hotel or back to their home, paying the fee before they left and us collecting our payment upfront when we got to wherever it was we were taken, or she would send one of us out from a phone description and we would have to take all the fees upfront and return her cut for the agency, before going home, if it was late.

She showed us around the reception room and downstairs to the ladies' lounge, which was not as smart as upstairs but was still nice and comfy and led through into the kitchen as well as having two toilets off it and a further dressing room in the back.

She waved us off, asking us to call in soon saying when we wanted to start and, with that, she shut the door after us as the phone began to ring on her desk.

While I was driving us back to my flat, Layla wound down the window to smoke and I said, 'I'm not sure I like her.'

'You only don't like her because she wants you to change your hair. She's all for the money, that one, but at least you know where you stand.' She took another drag and blew out the window.

'I don't know. It sounds more like working for MI5, with all that code bollocks, than being a whore.' I tapped the steering wheel, wondering if the police really were listening in to the phone calls.

'You want us to go to the other agency we found tomorrow for their interview and check them out too? Maybe they're different.'

I stopped tapping. Perhaps she was right. 'Well, it can't do any harm to go and see.'

Mr Fingers

Thursday: interview
Clients × 1 = Mr Fingers
1 × 2 hours = £250
– agency fee £70
Total = £180

Even after finding a place to park and feeding the meter, which took all my change, in a Kensington sidestreet, we arrived half an hour early for our interview the next day. We sat in a pub across the road and watched the door to the address we had been given. A smart older lady in a grey suit and carrying a pink handbag unlocked the door, which had a big swinging plaque jutting out above like a pub sign stating it was an escort agency and giving its phone number below. It was quite high up and not too clear, so I hadn't noticed it was there until we had sat down and were actually looking from across the street. The door was sandwiched between a shoe shop and a pub, and moments after it shut, a light went on above the shoe shop. The grey-clad figure who had just entered appeared briefly at the window and pulled down office blinds, which obscured our view.

'OK, honey, it looks like that's her,' Layla said, draining her fizzy drink very fast. 'Why don't they sell coffee in here? God, I need a coffee.' I checked my cheap little gold-plated work watch as I listened to her ramble. 'Right, nearly time. Better get moving then, better early than late, I suppose.'

We were buzzed in by the lady in grey and sat opposite her in her very grey and dark-green carpeted reception room. It looked like an office and had a smaller, office-like booth on the left side of the wall which contained two grey office chairs. You could just make them out through the opaque glass divide. The room was smart and clean but not as cosy as the other escort-agency office we had been in the day before. This one was slightly sterile-looking. There was also a door behind us, next to the one we had come in through, which I presumed was the girls' lounge.

'Hello, ladies. Five on the dot. I like punctuality in my ladies,' smiled the frail Ms Grey from over the desk. She might have looked small and fragile, but her eyes were like cut glass. Unlike the slightly sozzled Ms Lush the day before, this lady, I felt, saw everything and was as sharp as a tack.

Layla and I smiled back at her.

'So, I take it you have both worked before?' She didn't ask if we had been escorts, so there was no need to lie, and I had a feeling she had said on the phone to Layla that they only took on ladies who *had* worked before. I felt that no wouldn't have been the answer she was expecting to hear and we had both agreed beforehand to lie and be vague if she did ask.

Layla fidgeted and I said, yes, we had worked before, and Layla nodded.

'Right then. If you could fill out these forms, we'll get started. I have a few questions too.' She handed us each a printed list of questions on a sheet of paper mounted on a clipboard with a pen attached at the top.

Layla pulled her chair near to the desk and balanced the clipboard on the edge to fill it out. I saw Ms Grey squint at her as she did so, so I played safe and balanced mine on my knee. It had simple questions such as hair and eye colour, height, age, contact details, real name and work name – none of the personal questions in code we had been asked before. I handed my clipboard over to Ms Grey and Layla followed suit.

Ms Grey looked at them and then at me. 'Sorry – Scarlet? We already have a lady called that. How would you feel about being Suzy? We haven't had one of those.' And she put a line through my name and started to write over the top.

I just shrugged. 'How about Sarah?' I queried. I wasn't going to mention I had been a Shelly. I didn't want to be a Shelly again.

She looked up from her clipboard. 'No. We had one of those a few months back,' she said, and tapped her pen on the desk.

'Always thought you looked more like a Susan than a Sarah to me.' Layla shook her head as she said it.

'Susan?' I queried again.

'That will do, very girl-next-door.' Ms Grey scribbled it down and mumbled away. 'That will go down very well, very well, a Susan I can sell . . .'

As she wrote it down, without even looking at me, I doubted I had any choice now. She looked up and smiled at me. 'You know, if your hair was a bit lighter, you might do better. I'm always asked for blondes. I have quite a few clients looking for a lady like you – if you were a few years younger? You know, you could get away with it.' With that, she drew a line through my '22' and wrote '19'. 'You could get away with eighteen, but we will put you down at nineteen, since you have worked before. How's that, my dear?'

Layla squirmed again in her seat, and I gave her a poisonous look. What was wrong with her? I should be the one who was squirming: I was the one the old bag was calling 'my dear'.

I said that was fine. Then she looked over Layla's form and nodded.

'OK, ladies, it all looks fine. Now, do you do O levels?' She pulled out two index cards from a box on her desk, penned in our new names at the top of each and looked up.

'Yes,' said Layla and I in unison. Layla looked at me all smug, with her told-you-so look, and Ms Grey noted it and asked about A levels. That was a definite no from both of us.

She didn't ask if we kissed, but she did ask if either of us did any hardcore fetish things.

When Layla said yes, that she would piss on men and that watersports were fine by her, Ms Grey wrinkled her nose, scribbled away and then got up to show us the back room where the girls waited, stating they were a sit-in agency only and had no facilities for gents to 'stay', as it were.

The back room was a big black dark hole with a few shabby sofas and side tables. There was also a small, dirty kitchen which had leftover food on the counter and a sinkful of plates and, next to it, a poky little toilet. You had to wash your hands at the sink in the kitchen.

What a contrast to the smart, bright office out front.

The phone rang as she walked us back through from our quick tour and she gestured us to our seats as she answered it, looking at the call number displayed.

Layla and I looked at each other. She fidgeted again in her seat and I glared at her.

'Yes, I think I have the perfect girl for you – new, nineteen, green eyes, five foot five. Jonathan, you'll love her. She's a darling, just your type … can I call you back in a min? OK, speak soon.' Ms Grey put the phone down with a click and gave me a smile, the biggest one she had given me yet.

'Can you do a booking at 7 p.m.? He's really nice – one of my regular gents, has a house round the corner, so not too far away … I can get him to come in and meet you, see if you like him? It would only be two hours.'

I was already dressed and had brought my bag full of supplies with me, in case I needed anything, so I thought, why not give it a go and meet him? 'Sure, why not?' I said. I looked at Layla, who gazed at me nonplussed.

'Good, good. You can sign the contract later if you want to come back and work here permanently. Layla can sit in here and wait for you if you want. Neither of you have to start today … if you want to think about it?' Layla just looked at Ms Grey and then at me.

'That's OK. I have something to do tonight anyhow.' Layla smiled back at Ms Grey and then, looking at me, said, 'Call me when you're done. I'll feed the meter.' I nodded, a hundred things racing through my head at once.

Ms Grey started dialling call-back to the gent I was going to meet. I asked if it was all right if Layla and I left for a while, I'd come back in an hour, I needed to get something from the shops. She nodded and waved us off as she started chatting to the man on the other end of the line, singing my praises.

I poked Layla in the arm as we left and walked back to the car. 'What was with you in there? I know we ran out of coffee this morning, but you're not normally this grumpy or fidgety. Do you have ants in your pants or something?'

'I don't know – they're your damn knickers, the new pair you lent me this morning. I really need to get some laundry done, these damn things are too small.' She gabbled away, pulling at her skirt. 'You and your bloomin' dental-floss pants.'

Yep, someone needed a coffee all right. We emptied all her coin change into the parking meter to top it up and I dragged her to the nearest café for her fix.

'So what do you have to do tonight that's so damn important?' I grilled her as she sipped her coffee.

'Watch after you, you silly tart. I'm going to stand outside and, when you leave, trail you to find out where you end up. Then I can wait until you come out, to make sure you're safe.' She winked.

'You ... are a genie's arse.' I squeezed her arm. Now why hadn't I thought of that? 'What are you going to do for two hours waiting around? You'll be bored stiff.'

'W. H. Smith,' she said, slurping her coffee.

'W. H. Smith what?' I was puzzled. There was one on the corner that sold all sorts, but as we didn't know where

I was going to end up yet, I thought it a bit of a reach to use it as a stake-out point. 'It'll be closing soon.' I raised my eyes at her.

She nodded. 'I'm going to get a book or a magazine, then I'll have something to do while waiting for you. You can give me your car keys and I can sit in there if it gets too cold.' She finished her coffee and waved at the waiter for a second.

'Ahhh. We'd better get a couple of pocket A–Zs from there, too. At this rate, we'll need to know where we're going and where we're going to end up.' It was 5.45 p.m. and I was already a bag of nerves and not thinking too straight. At least someone was thinking about my safety.

After much rummaging through the shelves at W. H. Smith's to find Layla some interesting historical sex-industry-type books and a fashion mag, along with two pocket A–Zs that fit in our handbags, I went back to the agency office and was buzzed in. I took off my coat and sat waiting in the dark lounge with a few other girls who had now arrived.

One of the girls, Samantha, said hi and started to chat and be friendly, while the others sat and read or watched the television. The client I was going to see soon, so Samantha assured me, was a sweetheart, a very nice guy. She wished he saw girls more than just once, as she would have liked to have seen him again; she'd only seen him the once. They called him Mr Fingers, because he was a pianist. The agency sent the new, younger girls to him in order to get feedback, whispered Samantha to me, and then she bounded off to find her phone, which was ring-ing and had been recharging on a shelf somewhere in the messy kitchenette. Just before 7 p.m. I got a text from Layla, who was sitting in my car down the road: 'I think he's just about to arrive.' I read it as the doorbell sounded. All the girls started to get up until Samantha poked her head around the door and told everyone to sit back down, it was Mr Fingers for the new girl. I smiled, straightened myself up and went to see who this Mr Fingers was. I had had a Mr Magic Fingers before, but I had called him that for different reasons. I wondered if this one would be the same.

He was tall, very tall, but ordinary looking. I had to look up at him as I approached, as at only five foot six in my new heels, he must have been a good foot taller than me, but he looked friendly and smiled and said hello and bent to kiss my cheek. He was in a dark-blue suit and looked very smart even without a tie. I felt a bit uncomfortable in my tight cheap suit as all the other girls had nice dresses on – well, some did. Samantha's was all stretchy and shiny and made of a fabric that clung to every curve and rode up so you could see her stocking tops when she sat down. It looked a bit cheap on her and, as she wasn't the skinniest of girls, didn't flatter her at all.

We didn't chat much, just went through the motions: where I was from (I lied); so I was new? (I sort of lied again – well, I was new to being an escort, so that wasn't really a lie); how old was I? (I lied just like Ms Grey was doing now when she picked up the phone and told someone on the other end of the line that, yes, she had a tall, smartly dressed curvy blonde, called Samantha.)

Mr Fingers was at my side as I half-listened in to the

phone conversation. 'So, do you want to come with me?'

I said I would love to, looking over to Ms Grey, who just gestured that I should go. With that I dashed back into the lounge to grab my coat and bag. I don't know where my nerves had gone but I felt at ease in his company; he seemed OK, no bad vibes. He held the door open for me and led me down the street, chatting about the area and this and that. His house was only at the bottom of the street, and I saw Layla on the other side of the road pop into the same café we had been in earlier and watch me enter his home.

The building was narrow and the whole ground floor was one big, long wood-floored room, with the kitchen running along the right wall, a sofa in one corner and a sleek TV. Apart from that there was no furniture other than a gleaming black grand piano at the far end and a black four-legged stool. Wow! Now I was in mild shock – the place was like something out of one of those architectural books I had on my shelf at home. From the look of it, it had one bedroom on the mezzanine on the upper floor, reached by a winding glass staircase at the end of the room which went up the left-hand wall. I must have taken off my coat and handed it to him, and he got me a glass of water after asking what I wanted to drink. But, for the life of me, I wasn't paying much attention. The feel of the glass as he handed it to me brought me back to earth. 'Er, Susan?' He held out an envelope and I just looked at it.

'You should really ask for the fee upfront,' he said, and laid the envelope in my hand.

'Oh, yes, sorry,' I said, as I stuffed it in my bag.

He chuckled. 'I can tell you're new – you didn't even count it. Come here.' And with that he took away my glass and kissed me, and I ran my hand up his leg until I found a prominent bulge. And that was it. My jacket disappeared and my skirt was around my ankles in no time flat in the middle of the empty lounge. There was classical music coming from somewhere but I couldn't make it out and wasn't really interested. He bent down, scooped me up and strode to the piano, sitting me on the top facing him as he sat on the stool and peeled my knickers off down my legs, leaving my hold-ups on. Then he shrugged his jacket off, letting it fall to the floor. I had managed to undo most of my buttons by then, and my shirt fell open as he watched and he started to undo his too, saying, 'Take it off, and the bra. I want to watch you play with yourself.'

I undressed, watching him, and let my hand travel down my body. With my other hand supporting me, I obliged him, sticking two fingers up myself and panting a little. He unzipped his trousers in no time flat, still watching the progress of my fingers, which by now were wet from all the lube I had used, just in case. I hadn't known quite what to expect. He groaned at the squelching noises my pussy was making and, his trousers still round his ankles, he knelt heavily down on the stool and pushed away my fingers with his tongue and a long, exploring finger of his own. At that point I buckled and nearly slid off the piano and right on his face, in response to which he cupped his hands under my bum and lifted me back up until I was lying down on the polished black surface with my legs dangling down.

I felt dizzy and, after a few minutes of his mouth and fingers exploring, I really needed a good fucking. And really soon. I wriggled down until I was on his lap and kissed him. He was the one panting for breath now. I continued on my way down with rubber in hand from my stocking hold-up top and sucked it on to a springing, more than ready cock. It wasn't anything special, just a normal cock, but his intake of breath told me to take it easy, which for me, a thirty-minute girl, was not what I usually did. OK, slowly, I reminded myself; don't make him pop too soon. I eased down more slowly as he put his hand on the top of my head and shoved himself down my throat further, until I nearly gagged. Luckily, it didn't last until I turned blue, and he was soon trying to stand up and was pulling me up with him. He spun me around and bent me over the piano, running his hands down my legs and lifting me to enter. That was it: less than five minutes of frantic fucking in that position while holding my waist in place and he was spent. He sat down on the piano stool, all red and out of breath, puffing, sorry he couldn't last any longer, he had just needed me there and then on the piano. I stood up and walked over to get our discarded drinks, my knees wobbling slightly, and brought them back. He had recovered some of his breath. 'Sorry. I do make it to the bedroom, as a rule. God, you're tight. Sorry, I just lost it. Are you OK? I didn't bruise you on the hard edge …' He gasped, looking worried and stroking the piano top.

'No, I'm fine. Don't worry.' I giggled and sat on his lap, handing him his drink.

'I'm exhausted. We'd better get cleaned up and I can

walk you back,' he whispered in my ear. I looked over his shoulder and raised my arm to look at my watch; it wasn't that late.

'You want me to go? I have quite a lot of time left ... I can stay a bit longer. Ms Grey said as long as I was back in two hours ...' I picked up my knickers, which were at my feet, and hung them off my finger.

He laughed. 'No, that's OK. Now we're done you can go, that's the way it works. Even if it has been only thirty-five minutes. We'd better get you back, pretty one.'

We chatted for a bit about his house, as I was in no rush and he was in no real hurry to throw me out. It was nothing like a sauna or a brothel, where you had to run around and had a time restriction on what you could do. I resolved that I should try and make it last longer with the next one. I didn't want them complaining they didn't get value for money. If I could make a client come and be finished in thirty minutes, then surely I could work out how to make them last an hour or two.

We finished our drinks and he led me upstairs to the marble, monochrome bathroom, then he left me to clean myself up and have a shower and went off to find a bathrobe for himself.

Shortly afterwards Mr Fingers locked his door behind him and escorted me across the road and back to the agency. Across the road, I could see Layla in the front window, her head in her book. We were buzzed in. Ms Grey looked neither happy nor pleased until I walked over and gave her the envelope out of my bag. Then I stepped back, turning to my client and thanking him for walking me back. After that I left him to Ms Grey and slid off to the lounge. As I left I could hear Mr Fingers in the background say in a hushed voice, 'She's a little diamond . . .'

I sat down, still in my coat, and looked around. Samantha had gone but a few of the other girls were still there, so I flicked through a magazine until I heard the door go and my client leave. Ms Grey popped her head round the corner and beckoned me to the office. She looked very happy and handed me back the envelope, saying she had taken out her fee and the rest was mine, and if I wanted to work there she would love to have me. I only found out weeks later that she always gave Mr Fingers back the agency's cut, the introduction fee, as she called it, as thanks for making sure that the new girls put out and didn't just take the money for talking, doing nothing or 'social escorting', as it was called. No client really wanted a social-only escort and no agency could see the business sense or point in hiring one, or so the girls said in the lounge.

My new boss gave me a contract to sign then and there when I said that yes, I would like to work for her. The paper I signed listed ten points about my employment and basically said that I was an independent contractor and that the agency wasn't responsible for my taxes, as well as a few other little details. It was all rather long-winded, clarifying that I was being paid for time and companionship, just to cover the legal ass of the agency, I presumed.

The most ironic line was point 5a: The Escort also confirms that she is not nor ever has been a prostitute –

though it was closely followed by point 5b: The Escort also agrees that under no circumstances will she use the agency's facilities to promote prostitution in any way.

Considering that no escort agency would hire a girl unless she said she had worked before, it was a farce. And Ms Grey sent us to hotel rooms and houses all the time while, according to our contract point 8d: The Escort will not date the client privately nor go to a private residence or hotel room. Failure to adhere to this instruction will result in immediate dismissal. It all meant the contract wasn't really much of a contract.

The only useful part was really for Ms Grey, the agency's information about the girl at the bottom. You had to fill out your 'Full-time occupation' (if you didn't, either 'student' was put in, if you were under twenty-one, or 'secretary' if you were over); 'Status', which had 'Married/Single', and the 'Married' was scrubbed out already on the photocopied document, so everyone who signed it had single status whether you were or not. Then there was a big space for Hobbies and shorter ones for Height/Colour of Hair/Colour of Eyes and a space at the bottom that said 'Signed by'.

After signing in my new name and a scribble as a last name and after much prompting to put 'student' and a fake height of two inches taller than I was, Ms Grey put me down for some shifts that week, starting the next day. I asked whether I should bring a dress in case any of the gents wanted to take me out on the town and after answering she said that I could go home. She said to be back at 6 p.m. prompt the next day and added that I couldn't leave after a booking again unless it had started after 9 p.m. I could come back after a late booking if I wanted to try and get another, but they closed at 1 a.m. With that, she waved me out of the door. I stood on the pavement and looked around, a bit bewildered. I had just earned £180 (he had paid me £250 – I had looked in the bathroom when I had gone to clean up – so the agency or, should I say Ms Grey, had taken £70 out), and I had only gone in for an interview! Not bad for a day's work. She let me keep the money this time. She would keep the fee for my first official client as a two-week deposit, in case I didn't stay.

I walked up the road to fetch Layla, thinking that I was going to like this escort lark. Having glanced at Mr Fingers' front door across the street, I knocked on the window of the café opposite for Layla to come out. She looked all dazed and confused. She had been so en-grossed in her new book she hadn't seen us leave the house over the road.

'So, how did it go?' she asked as I drove us back to my warm, safe flat, which was forty-five minutes away in north London. I told her all about it and what had happened, and she was happy for me but said she didn't think she liked Ms Grey that much. She would go and work at the other place, the one we had had an interview at the day before, with Ms Lush. It looked quieter and had less business, we agreed, but Ms Lush paid more. The rate started at £270 and the agency cut was the same at £70 but that still left the escort with £200. Layla said she could always give me the extra for petrol money for driving her to and from the other agency and, as Ms Lush's didn't shut till 2 a.m., it would work out perfectly.

We could test out both at the same time and see which was the better one to work for.

The next day I called the sauna and spoke to Emma, as I wasn't working that day. I fibbed and said I had an emergency in my family and that I had to take some time off and would call them when I was back, to see if they would have me on the rota again. I didn't want to burn all my bridges, in case the agency didn't turn out as I planned. At least then I could fall back on working at the sauna. I certainly wasn't going to extend that bridge back to stripping, that was for sure.

8. *Sit-in Agency: A Bad John*

At the agency, if you went out after 9 p.m. and you had been taken out from the office or the client paid by credit card over the phone (so your fee to the agency had been paid), you were free to go home. If he paid in cash and you had been sent to him, you had to stop by the office and drop off the fee before going home. If you came back to sit and see if you could get another booking, it made the receptionist happy – she would at least have some girls to sell in the evening, when it was busier – but on the flip side, if the other girls hadn't been so lucky to be picked that night, you were considered greedy. Most girls, unless they were really desperate for the cash to pay a standing bill or upcoming rent, didn't come back after a 9 p.m. booking, and if they had had a slightly earlier one and had to come back they normally put on a very grumpy face when they said hello to any gent who came through the door in order not to be picked again. I, on the other hand, unless it had been a hard or long booking, would always go back and sit until closing time. I was doing quite a few early shifts and the girls felt sorry for me; no one gave me the cold shoulder because of it. Who's going to give you a hard time and call you a money-grabbing bitch when you're doing the bad shifts and cleaning up their mess in the kitchen and lounge from the night before?

There were a few things that made the agency happy.

Money, obviously: the more clients you could see in a week, the more money you brought in. Repeat custom: I always gave the gent the agency's card and wrote my name on the back, so when they called they knew who to ask for. It's surprising, but after a few months a client could completely forget your name and then give a description that didn't fit you at all. Another tactic was to ask my regular clients to call before they came in just to check I was there. My name popping up on the phone all the time made the agency think I was in demand. In Ms Grey's mind, popular meant good and repeat custom, so being on the receptionist's mind and in her ear all the time was no bad thing, especially if there were no new girls to push on the phone.

New girls are always popular for the first two weeks – not that they are really new and fresh, as most escorts did the rounds and would work at different agencies in order to cream off from new-girl status. There were very few actual new girls. The agency owner would always push the new girls on the phone and talk them up as a good thing so that the girl was busy and earned enough money to pay her deposit. She would also be more inclined to stay if she was earning well. She would be pushed at every client for at least two weeks or until there was another new girl to take her place. After that, it was sink or swim. She would know the lie of the agency's land by then and, if she was good, she would have picked up some regulars of her own for the weeks or months ahead. If she hadn't got the hang of saying hello, didn't like it or was earning badly, she would normally leave and try another agency or give up altogether.

I had come to hate being a new girl; it wasn't my strong point. Being new girl anywhere is never any fun, is it? And in the sex industry it's twice as bad; you always got more of the grotty clients as a new girl. In the past, that was what had happened in the brothel, then in the sauna and, now, with the agency, it wasn't any different. There are always clients who like new girls and will only see a new girl; they're always looking out for someone who knows nothing, someone they can take advantage of, and they'll try and get things from her that other girls won't do. If a girl hasn't been around a bit, she won't know any different, she won't know that there are certain things you don't have to do, things that other girls don't do because of the health risks.

Kissing was still seen as a big taboo, and no one would do anything unprotected. If they did, the other girls would talk about it in the lounge with disdain and say that they would tell their clients, 'If I wanted to catch something by doing something like that or was that desperate, I'd go stand on a street corner or work in an alley behind King's Cross station.' The common consensus in the lounge was that if you did oral without protection no one would sit near you in case they caught something. It was all very snotty, but it was the same in most agencies, from what I heard; only the cheaper girls did that sort of thing. As the agencies had a pretty fixed list of clients, most of the gents knew the score; it was very rare to come across a client who hadn't been to an agency before. The majority even automatically handed you a £20 tip for cab fare at the end when you were ready to leave, without having to be asked.

If a client was new to an escort agency, he would normally be introduced by a friend; it was unusual to get a walk-in off the street. Clients rarely pushed for a kiss mouth-to-mouth – you were lucky if you got a peck on the cheek – and asking for oral without a rubber was virtually unheard of. With all the government-sponsored information on HIV and Aids over the past years, everyone was very paranoid. One of the girls, who was a nurse, even confessed to using a rubber surgical glove if she had to give hand relief, which, although it raised a laugh or two, wasn't dismissed outright by the girls in the lounge. And I thought I was paranoid about my health!

Bad John

Friday: first shift at an escort agency 6 p.m.–1 a.m.

Clients x 2 = Bad John, Mr Old English

+ cab-fare tip = £20 (Mr Old English)

2 x 2 hours = £500

Total = £520

– agency fee £140

– cab fares + £6 (there and back to Park Lane)

Total = £368

'You have a booking for 7 p.m. with one of our regulars. He wants you at the hotel round the corner. Here is the info ... you need to collect the fees, as he doesn't do credit cards.' Ms Grey handed me a Post-it note with the hotel address, the client's name, 'John', a room number and the time written on it.

'He shouldn't need you long, and I'll need you back

promptly, as I might have another booking for you later.'
With that, I was dismissed, and she turned her attention
to another girl who had walked in after me.

I left the agency and walked up the street. Ms Grey had
given me directions as I headed out and it wasn't very
far to the hotel. I turned up at the shabby hotel door at
7 p.m. precisely and knocked, only to be confronted with
a stern-looking, broad blond man in his early forties.

'You're late. I said 7 p.m.' was all he said, as he ushered
me into the small room and locked the door behind me.
I looked at my watch, which took my attention away
from the lock. I wasn't late according to my watch, so I
looked at the bedside clock, and that said five minutes
past.

'I'm terribly sorry, my watch must be slow,' I apolo-
gized, even though I knew I wasn't late at all. Getting the
time right was something I was very conscious of: one
minute late calling in, and it would cost me. As the agency
would want another £70 fee off me whether the client
paid me for extra time or not, the time was always on my
mind. Girls were always trying to diddle agencies out
of money, or so the agencies thought (and most of the
time they were right). The agency didn't really care, they
just wanted the money. I set my clocks and phone to the
speaking clock because of it. A good escort was expected
to be on time, to call to check in and call when she left
a booking so the agency knew she was on her way back
and when they could stop the clock, as it were. I got the
impression that keeping on a girl whose timekeeping
was bad was unprofessional, and that an unprofessional
escort was either not very employable, only worth giving

the worst shifts to or, even worse, the worst clients, the ones none of the other girls wanted.

He interrupted me with a slight smile, bringing me back to earth. I was hoping he had changed his mind about hiring me. No such luck. He said, 'Well, you're here now. Turn around and let's get a good look.'

I did a slow turn on the spot. I didn't like his tone, but had been told he was a regular, so it was best just to smile. Hopefully, I would be out of there soon.

There was a small shower room at the foot of the queen-sized bed, and not much room around the bed for any other furniture. It was a very small, damp and probably cheap room; it was obvious he wasn't into impressing a girl. His casual appearance, the location and his unshaven face spoke volumes.

He came around and plonked his ample frame down on the bed next to me. I turned to face him.

'So, are you a good girl?' he said, raising an eyebrow and reaching out, shoving his hand up my skirt and poking and grasping at my knickers underneath. That was a bit of a shock, but it really shouldn't have been, considering I had met his type before. He tried to push the folds of my long coat out of the way so he could look at what he was doing and nearly made me topple over, getting his hands caught up in my suspenders as he did so. He didn't look too happy that he was being impeded by my underwear.

I grinned down on his thinning hair and then, looking at the opposite wall, said, 'I hope so. I take it you want me to stay then?' his hand still groping away under my coat and skirt.

He lifted my skirt up as I stood and took a small step back. Soon I was against the wall, and he pinged my suspenders. Ouch, that hurt a bit. My indrawn breath made him grin. It was obvious he got off on it.

'You're new, right?' he queried, and I nodded. 'Yeah, you'll do. Take all that off under there. Leave the skirt on.' He grunted as he started to undo his belt buckle and leaned back on the bed. I really didn't like his tone *at all*. He was obviously looking for a submissive girl and expecting me to do whatever he ordered. I didn't usually mind if a man wanted to be in control, and I had dealt with lots of men who liked young girls before, but I didn't like his rough manner. I wasn't as sub as he obviously wanted me to be, and that was going to mean trouble.

'Umm, sure, but I have to call the agency first to check in and let them know I have the fees.'

It was my subtle hint to him to pay me, but he just grunted and said to make it a quick call. I fished my phone out of my bag, keeping an eye on the door and noting that as he had now got up from the bed and was standing between me and the door, I wasn't in the best position to leave in a hurry if I had to. I smiled again and made the call to check in with my boss, Ms Grey.

'Yes, I'm here,' I answered the disembodied voice on the other end. 'No, he hasn't paid me yet.' I hadn't been asked but had been told to say that by one of the girls in the office to prompt the client to pay the fee.

I turned to my non-paying client and smiled again. He said loudly, so it could be heard on the other end of the phone, 'I'll pay her later.' And he reached for his zip.

'It's OK, I heard. John's fine. He'll pay you at the end.' Having said that, Ms Grey hung up.

I looked at my phone and then back at my unpleasant client, who was now lolling on the bed. Turning my phone off, I slid it into my pocket and started to walk around the bed, on my way to hang my coat up on the back of the door. Well, Mr Fingers had been great and had paid. This one wasn't great, but if she said he would pay, then, fingers crossed, he would.

'Where're you going?' He grabbed for my arm as I made my way past.

'Hang my coat up.' I shrugged it off, and he let go of my arm. I hung my coat up. At least I was on the side near the door now. I put my bag on the floor, again near the door, and pushed my knickers, stockings and suspenders down as quickly as I could to please him. Then I kicked off my shoes, keeping everything in one pile on top of my bag, just in case I needed to grab it all and make a quick exit.

He was now standing at the foot of the bed, towering over me in the small room, his trousers around his ankles.

'OK. Get on all fours on the bed,' he ordered. 'I want to see that little ass in the air for me.' He grinned. 'Let's see what you got under that skirt,' he said, as he rubbed his crotch bulge through his boxer shorts. I reached for the rubber that had fallen out of the top of my stocking before I bent over the bed as he had asked.

'Like this?' I queried, lifting up my skirt to give him a view and tucking it into the waistband.

'Yeah,' he grunted, shoving a cupped hand between my legs. I could feel his weight on the bed behind as he poked a thumb roughly up me. 'Nice tight pink cunt. I'm going to enjoy fucking you open,' he said in a sinister whisper over my shoulder as he bent over me, trying to shove more fingers up me as he did so. I wriggled forward a bit, away from him and his probing fingers, as they were hurting a bit. I hadn't had a rough customer in quite some time. I started to turn over, wanting to divert his attention.

'You want to watch me play with my twat? I'm getting a bit wet.' I grinned up at his expectant face. Two could play at his game.

He leaned back, leering, as I turned over on to my back and started to unbutton my blouse and take my bra off, my skirt still hitched up around my waist.

'You are a bit wet, but we can fix that,' he said, grabbing a fistful of the dowdy bedcover and starting to rub away at my crotch before I could stop him. That didn't make me at all happy, as he was rubbing off all my lube, but he looked pleased at causing me discomfort. Putting his hands down his boxer shorts and pulling his cock out, he played with himself as he watched me finger myself, laid out beneath him on the bed.

'Come and suck it, slut.' He proffered his big ruddy-red cock at me, now standing at the side of the bed. 'Come and suck my big fat cock.'

I crawled across, the rubber still in my hand and, just before I was about to put it on with my mouth and hands, he grabbed my hair and pulled me up. Looking into my eyes, he grunted, 'No, not fucking yet, just want to shove it down your tight throat.'

He let go of my hair and I said, 'Deep throat? Sure, I

love to suck rubber.' I smiled and nodded away as if I hadn't understood that he wanted me to suck it without. 'Go on, make me gag with your big long cock,' I breathed, all the while sucking the rubber on as quickly as I could, so I was mumbling the words over his average-sized dick before he could realize what I was doing.

'That's not what I meant . . . not with.' He grabbed the back of my head and shoved his cock further in, slamming his crotch in my face. His balls were slapping me under the chin while he groaned away. 'Yes, you little whore . . . ahhh . . . going to be your fresh pink twat next . . . ahh . . . Ooopen you up.' He didn't last long; he was soon on the brink, which was good as I was having trouble breathing. He might not have been overly endowed, but sheer force was knocking the breath out of me.

'Yes, going to stretch you open now,' he grunted.

Yeah, go ahead and try, I thought. He had no chance if I relaxed my muscles; the amount of better-endowed men I have had in the past, it was very unlikely he could stretch anything down there. If he was aiming to hurt me, it wasn't going to work. Flipping me backwards quickly, he grabbed my legs and hauled me to him, impaling me just as quickly and ramming away, still carrying on his tirade of abuse.

'Bet you haven't had big cock like this before . . . ahhh . . . fresh cunt . . . does that hurt? . . . ha ha.' He grabbed at my tits and I breathed heavily so he thought it did. He didn't seem bothered that I wasn't moving much, that I was just pinned under him, as he was more intent on what he was doing, as if I wasn't really there at all other than as a hole to fill. He was plain vile. I had met his type in the past, he just wanted a body to use, and I knew the quickest way to get out of there was to give him what he wanted and be shot of him. The more I fought, the more it would turn him on. I groaned as if I was in a bit of pain, even though I had relaxed to stop him hurting me so much. I was a bit numb by then anyway, thank goodness, from the rubbing. I had a feeling I was going to have bruises the next day as it was, and I didn't want to make it worse by tensing up.

I wiggled about and moaned a bit more as if he was hurting me more than he actually was. The sadistic sod seemed to like it so I thought it would make him come quicker and I could leave sooner. I was right.

'Yeah … ahhh … serves you right for not sucking my cock right … ahh … you're only useful for fucking and coming over, aren't you, you dirty little whore?' With that he pulled out, whipping off the condom, and exploded all up my body across my chest. I lifted my hands just in time to stop it getting on my face and in my hair but it had covered most of me all over.

But that wasn't the annoying bit, the annoying thing was the fact he had taken the rubber off and I hadn't had a chance to 'accidentally' ping it as I took it off his sensitive cock after he had come. My chance of retribution had been lost.

He huffed and plonked himself down on the edge of the bed, wiping his cock on the bedcovers as I sat up and started wiping his come off my body with one hand, the come I hadn't been expecting. He got up and opened the bedside drawer after that, taking out a stack of £20 notes and throwing them on the bed at me.

'There, you can go now,' he sneered, not even looking at me, and fishing up his boxer shorts from the floor and pulling them on.

'OK. Can I just use the bathroom to clean up and – ' I was interrupted with a scowl as I gathered up the cash on the bed with my clean hand.

'No. Just go, get out of my sight.' He reached for the TV remote and pointed it at the TV high up on the wall in the corner facing the foot of the bed. I shoved the cash in my bag and reached in the bathroom for a towel, rubbing myself dry as I picked up my clothes and put them on as quickly as I could. I was glad I had a change of outfit back at the agency, and that I could have a wash there. He took no notice of me, just carried on watching the news as I put on my coat to leave. I just wanted to get out of there, so I murmured a 'Goodbye' as I opened his hotel-room door and walked out without looking back.

A shiver went down my back as I stood in the dark corridor wiping my hands with an antiseptic wet wipe from my bag. He was a regular client? Why hadn't she warned me? She must have known what he was like before she sent me to him. What was this, some sort of escort baptism of fire? Hook you in with a good client and then see if you could stick it by giving you a vile one?

I walked back to the agency feeling a bit confused. I hated to think what he would have done to me or tried to make me do if I had been green and truly new to the game as he had expected. Then again, I would probably have done what he wanted and been a good girl for him, if I hadn't known any better. If that made me a bad girl, then good, at least he wouldn't pick me again.

I was buzzed into the agency and put the £70 so-called introduction fee on the desk.

'OK?' Ms Grey said, looking up from her magazine and seeing my frown.

'I don't think he liked me at all, and he was a bit rough.' I didn't bother sitting down, as I just wanted to go to the bathroom for a wash. I could still smell his sweat on me – eau de vile client is never one of my favourites.

'Umm, yes, he just called. It's OK, you won't be going to him again.' She picked up the money on the desk. 'He can be a bit choosy; not many girls like him or suit his needs.' She smiled up at me. 'Bit of a difficult one, John, but a regular client, like to keep him sweet, always wants to see the new girls.'

She was distracted now by counting the money I had given her and noting it down in her book.

'Oh, you have another outcall at 9.30 p.m., a hotel on Park Lane. Can't have you being late for this one now, can we? Nice old reg, he's a darling, you won't have any problems … Think you'd better call me when you're there and then call to confirm when you're in the room.' She looked down again at her book and scribbled away. I took the silence as my cue to leave and go and clean up. I didn't bother trying to argue that I hadn't been late turning up, as John had obviously complained to her. Too right I was going to call her when I arrived at the next one – so she knew I wasn't late.

The night dragged on. Ms Grey was right: I had no problems with the English chap later on and was back in time to kick my shoes off and watch some TV before leaving when the agency shut to go and pick Layla up from her agency, which was five minutes down the road.

'So, how was your first day, love?' It was 1.05 p.m. and I was driving us back to my flat in north London.

Layla rolled down the window and puffed on her cigarette. 'Yeah, surprisingly OK. I had an old English guy early on – that made the Lush happy – and spent the rest of the night chatting to a girl called Tandy.' She took another puff and blew the smoke out of the window. 'Smart cookie, that one, was going on about ways to get mortgages, shares and such, very interesting.' She stared off into the distance.

'Hello? Earth calling Layla, you looking to buy a house?' This was the first I had heard of it; she had mentioned renting her own place but not buying a pile of bricks.

She drew on her fag and puffed it out again. 'No, no. It was just that listening to Tandy made me think that I should save more, like you do. Where does our money go?' She rattled on while puffing away the whole trip back. 'I mean, you no sooner make it than it's spent. "The more you make, the more you tend to spend," Tandy said earlier, and I think she's right . . .'

After a week at the agency I was doing well, despite getting some clients I didn't like. I was new, so I was bound to get a few bad ones picking on me; I knew that. Both Layla and I did well; even she was surprised how well. I had earned more in the agency that first week than in two months at the sauna. I was definitely not going back there now. I no longer needed to work like that; I was enjoying working as an escort. I felt I had more in common with the girls at the agency than I had with those at the sauna or the stripclub, or even the brothel where I had started. Unlike at the sauna, in the agency no one thought it was strange that I read books rather than magazines. Other girls were reading even bigger books than I was. It wasn't snobbery; I just felt that I fitted in better. I didn't feel I stood out as much, as most of the girls in the agency were around my age, single without kids and dressed smartly too. I didn't have to dress down or plainly to come into work out of fear I might get picked on or that rumours would start that I was earning too much and probably fiddling the house, because I had expensive, nice-looking stuff.

At the agency, flash was all the rage. Not all of it was elegant, though. Most girls had designer this and that, and the amount of money they earned was a way to show how good they were, and the designer brands a way to show the other girls how much they could afford to spend. Louis Vuitton handbags were rife; no one could get away with a fake, as all the girls knew what a real one looked like, and a fake was worse than a cheap bag, as everyone thought you were pretending to be something you weren't. Shoes and watches, too, were a mark of how well you did. Everyone at the agency knew, for example, that a real Gucci bangle watch was £395, and if you were wearing a fake, they knew it and would take the piss out of you. If a new girl started and had on a real Gucci watch, the girls at the agency would know she was one of them and would be more likely to talk to her. The older girls would be far less likely to try it on. With a non-Gucci new girl, they thought they could get away with hassling her, giving her a sob story and asking her to loan them money, making her go to the shops for their fags, making tea or cleaning up their mess in the kitchen, and so on. They knew they wouldn't be able to get away with it if the girl had worked before and knew the score. Having the same designer things as the other girls made a statement that she would know their bullshite and wouldn't put up with it.

I didn't have the designer flash, I've never really liked it, but the fact that I dressed smartly confused most, and responding, 'Yes, I would love one,' and adding, 'if you're making it?' with a big smile to anyone saying 'Tea?', kept most of the bitches at bay, and stopped them from saying, 'Make me one too,' and leaving me to make it for them. I didn't need a Vuitton bag as protection. It all sounds a bit silly but, when you have a bunch of girls in one smoky room for hours on end, subtle little things like that can mean a lot. I quickly worked out that there was a hierarchy among the girls in agencies too, just as in the other houses and saunas. It wasn't much different. The bling was nothing to do with style or how well off you were and everything to do with an escort's status in the agency. It was more about being bitchy than snobbery.

The girls who had been there longest commanded the most respect from the others. After all, they were the ones you could go to, the ones who had all the information and gossip you might need. The girls who worked more than the others and earned more, the top girls, were given more leeway and better shifts, and the owners were more likely to trust them and stand up for them if anything went wrong, as they were the ones making the most for the agency, too. If you let one girl get to you and walk all over you, then others would too. It wasn't just the clients you had to keep happy and keep an eye on, you had to look out for the girls and the owners as well. Whoever says being a hooker is easy money doesn't know *what* they're talking about.

9. *Things that Go Hump in the Night*

A week flew by and, so far, I had no reason to call my personal sex-toy Tony for physical relief. We had spoken on the phone a few times in the mornings; the phone sex wasn't that great, but I was realizing that, as big, powerful and macho as he made out he was, he was actually more submissive than I thought. It wasn't a bad thing, but it did mean that I did most of the dirty talk, which got him beating off but didn't do much for me. I had an inkling he was hiding something – after all, working and dealing all the time with men who keep the secret of seeing working-girls gives a girl a sexual sixth sense of how men lie. I eventually got him to admit that he had a wife. He sounded a bit put out that I wasn't bothered he was attached, which I guess was his male pride needling him.

I saw the fact that he had a missus as a good thing, not a bad thing at all. It meant he wouldn't be bothering me too much or get too clingy. Not that he would have anyway, knowing that I was a working girl and what I did, but him being married meant I had a better hold over him than he had over me. He was in no position to mess me around or tell anyone and – best of all – he was less likely to turn into a stalker. It wasn't like I wanted a relationship with him, it was more his gorgeous body I wanted and, since my previous playmate had disappeared – the last man in my semi-private life had been an older gent, who had taken me to Venice and then disappeared into the phone hell of 'The number you have dialled is no longer in use' – I needed a replacement. This time, rather than intellect, a brain to keep me stimulated, I thought I might as well go for brawn, and Tony, who spent all his time in the gym and had a chest that needed custom-made shirts it was so broad and biceps bigger than my waist, was definitely brawn.

I didn't tell him I was working as an escort until the week after I had started, once I knew I was going to stick at it. He just presumed I was still at the sauna, although he had made some comments about better places I could work and was a bit worried about my safety. When I did tell him I was working as an escort, he sounded quite impressed, as if I had taken his advice, but he wasn't quite so impressed when I said I was too busy to see him for a week or so, and that I would call him at the end of the week and come and pick him up. He didn't have a car.

Layla was going off back down south the following weekend, so it was the perfect time to get him around and have some fun. I was hoping he would take me out of my paranoid mood and, if the week ahead was anything like the last, on my two days off I was probably going to need some good sex to keep me sane.

It hadn't been long, but I had forgotten how big he really was. I picked him up from the tube station, and it was as if a gorilla was climbing into my passenger seat, a huge silverback, and he looked even bigger in the small con-fines of my hatchback. I was seeing him in the daylight for the first time, and his cheeky killer-wattage smile shone. He was more relaxed, too, which wasn't surprising, considering that the last time we had met was in the sauna, where he hadn't wanted to be in the first place. We chatted on the way to mine, but my mind was elsewhere, especially when he put his hand on my knee. I had to remove it, reluctantly, as it was getting in the way when I had to change gear.

He was looking at me suspiciously out of the corner of his eye. He only stopped frowning when I told him to stop sulking, which, as I was wound a bit tight and thinking only of getting my hands on him, came out as more of a command than a request. That brought an even bigger, pearly-white grin to his face – another indication that he was really a bit submissive. But after a grotty week of being paid to be at men's beck and call, and of getting some of the not-so-nice gents, as I was still being sold over the phone as the new girl at the agency, it made a nice change and it felt good to have a man under my command. At my front door, I dropped one of my gloves on purpose, which had him bending down to pick it up for me before I could open the door. Yep – definitely submissive tendencies.

After a whistlestop tour of my compact flat and a blatant kneading of Tony's shoulders, slyly using the excuse that he felt to me as if he needed a massage, I got him to dispense with his clothing in no time at all. It wouldn't have been difficult in any case; I could have used any excuse. I had his huge black body beneath my hands and at my mercy before I remembered to take more than my heels off.

As I was kneeling at his side, massaging the tight

muscles in his back and sliding my hands along his bulging thighs, his hand snuck under my skirt and one of his sneaky fingers probed at the gusset of my damp thong, stroking along the edge of the fabric and teasing it aside to slip underneath, then fondling the damp lips it found. It wasn't difficult to wiggle back and impale myself on it, which caught his attention and allowed me to turn him over so I could rubber him up to suck his cock. His girth looked eye-wateringly good and, from what I remembered, it would grow from its semi-hard state to become a full, rigid prick in a matter of seconds. If, that was, I could get to it. Tony's attention was at present fully focused on my wet pussy. He licked the finger that had been probing my cunt and was now intent on laying me down and licking me out.

Surrendering was no chore. His huge frame bunched between my thighs and pushed my knees apart for better access, and he covered my pussy with his hot mouth and sucked, then settled to flicking my clit with his tongue, then to probing with more than one finger, stretching my hole as he went, until I came over his face and all over his fingers.

He stretched up, looking supremely happy with himself. I was contemplating jumping on his cock, and I grabbed a rubber from under my pillow, one of a few I had put there that morning, ready. I had him rubbered up in no time and lying beneath me before he realized that I now wanted his cock to fuck and not to suck. After a moment squatting above his erection, it was easy to slide down his girth, as I was so wet. I squeezed my cunt muscles, inching down nearly all the way but holding off, just, to rock forward on my knees and hoarsely whisper that I wasn't going to let him come until I wanted him to. That earned a groan from deep in the tense mass of dark, contrasting body beneath me and a twitch in his cock as he fought to buck up to bury himself further.

Time was a novelty I hadn't had at my disposal in a long time. I had meant what I said: I wasn't going to let him come until I had him where I wanted him, and where I wanted him wasn't just in a position to make me come – I wanted a full, knee-trembling, knock-the-breath-out-of-me, didn't-know-where-I-was orgasm, and that, I knew, took time, time to wind me up a few notches to make me dizzy and make my brain flood with all the dopamine I would produce, so that the wave would wash over me and I wouldn't be able to think straight.

Coming for me is a brief, pleasant sensation of pins and needles that skitters up my body like a wave. It's like being wrapped in a warm blanket that makes my body pulse and the blood rush in my ears. An orgasm is, for me at least, a different sensation, a different kind of climax. It's more like an explosion that makes me convulse and my eyes roll in my head; it makes me painfully sensitive all over. It didn't happen very often – most of the time a quick screw and coming would satisfy me – but even a vibrator can't make me orgasm. Fingers crossed that Tony had the potential I thought he had. Perhaps I would be in luck.

I pinned his arms above his head and leaned over him, rolling my hips, stroking his cock with my internal muscles, gripping hold and riding him, easing back to slow the pace when he tensed and nearly came. As I rocked back on my heels, he felt a good fit beneath me, so I swivelled, sitting on his cock in a reverse cowgirl position, my feet together, heels pressing back on his balls. I lifted up, ready to slide down even tighter than before on his pulsing dick. I felt him push up on to his arms, watching me slide down on him. It wasn't long before he wriggled up on to his knees so I could bend over doggie-style, holding on to the bedhead as he started to pound away.

He had a powerful arm around my waist and was lifting my knees off the bed so that I fit him better as if I weighed nothing at all. I fingered my clit to bring myself off as he pushed harder. 'Harder,' I urged, pushing back as he thrust, and that was all it took before I felt a spark go off. I convulsed and groaned as my pussy tightened around him, locked in the orgasm I wanted. I felt the heat as he came.

It was quite some minutes until we both had our breath back and my knees were strong enough to be able to stand. I stretched like a cat and, as I always did after sex, hopped off the bed to go to the bathroom, not giving it a second thought.

'Where are you going?' He sat up, looking and sounding shocked.

I looked over my shoulder. I shrugged, still a bit dizzy. 'Shower,' I replied. Mmm, a nice hot shower ... after all, he had sweated buckets, all over me, and I felt sticky. I wasn't thinking too clearly. My head was fuzzy with cotton wool.

I turned around to face him, leaning against the door-frame naked, my arms crossed, and only then thinking to ask him if he wanted to use the bathroom first.

He shook his head, still looking put out, as I turned and padded to the room next door, murmuring over my shoulder, 'Put the kettle on, will you, for me? We have plenty of time for round two before I have to drop you back at the station.'

I planned to tie him to the bed next and to tease him into oblivion in thanks. I didn't think he would mind, even if it did take a couple of hours. Now, where was that blindfold Layla had bought me for a funny birthday present?

Christmas Escape

I spent as little time as I could possibly get away with back down south for Christmas with the folks, all so I could get back to the agency for the New Year, as Ms Grey had said it would be busy.

I wasn't used to keeping normal hours now, and I found being up in daylight very strange, much to the amusement of my family, who kept on trying to wake me up at some stupid hour in a normal person's morning, flinging open the curtains in the spare room in which I was sleeping and calling me lazy, which didn't help my mood. Although it was Christmas and I hadn't seen them all in a while, I couldn't wait to leave and get back to my blacked-out flat in quiet north London, where people didn't just drop by without calling first and expect you to be sunny and bright all the time.

I was getting slightly paranoid again. I would avoid crowds if I could, and it wasn't just crowds – going out at all in daylight made me anxious for some illogical reason, and it would take some deep breaths to stop my hand shaking on the outside-door handle before I could open it to get to my car. It seemed the paranoia I used to have when working at the brothel had returned full force, but I hadn't really noticed I was pulling away from people and cutting off friends.

As her family wasn't in England, Layla had stayed in London, which gave me a great excuse to get back. I said I needed to keep her company, but that didn't help much, as my mother kept on saying that I should have brought her down to stay over Christmas too. Talk about fuss and kill you with kindness. And I like Layla far too much as a friend to subject her to my lot. Layla got off easy, staying in town and working at her agency on Christmas Day, not that she was busy.

I was glad when I got back to London. I snuck back before New Year, saying I had to get back as friends were having a party but spending the evening in the dark, reading by candlelight, while Layla was out with a guy she had met in a bar, a musician in a small band who also had a nine-to-five job. It sounded serious. I hadn't known her date before – Layla had always lectured about the evils of giving it away for free, ever since some psycho ex- she split up with after I had met her – so I didn't press and ask her much about him.

After New Year I found that the girls at the agency were just as crazy as those in the brothel, and the clients were even more risky. I never really knew where I would end up after a booking, but it never occurred to me that the agency might not know where I was all the time. The guys I saw may have been pervs, or a bit slimy, but on the whole they were nice enough, and none had been too much trouble. You had the occasional drunk, or one or two you thought might be a bit high, but none had been violent. I was more paranoid that people, my family even, might find out what I was doing. I didn't want to worry my mother.

It was only later that I realized I had started to become agoraphobic and a bit depressed. Just working as an escort and not doing anything other than that can make you go a bit crazy. You keep such abnormal hours, it can be very lonely. It just becomes easier to lock people out, not to do other things that could get in the way of earning money, and that in turn feeds the money addiction. I don't fare well without novelty and change in my life, and being stuck in a rut, being paid for sex night after night, can drive you a bit mad, and you don't even know it's happening. And it wasn't just me; I was noticing it in other girls too.

One late afternoon, as I was watching TV while eating my breakfast, Layla padded into the lounge and said, 'My god, you're white – when was the last time you saw daylight? You look like a vampire.' I laughed it off.

'You're looking pale yourself, missus,' I said, and gave her a poke as she sat down. She was right though, I was looking pale, but that didn't bother me: I was still getting picked. The clients liked me white. Who needed a tan?

But in another way, maybe there was a problem. It must have been at least three months since I'd seen the sun. By the time I left the flat to drive to the agency it was always late afternoon and getting dark, and I went to the supermarket late in the evening. Layla was still sleeping on my couch, and to stop the daylight waking her when she eventually got to sleep, we had taped bin bags over the windows to stop it coming through the flimsy curtains. I'd done the same in my bedroom, and masked off the small window in the front door, which gave the only light in the hallway, so no one could look in. The bathroom didn't have a window and the kitchen was in the shade in the afternoon. No wonder my body clock was totally screwed up.

Layla was trying to earn as much as she could before going back to another term at uni, and I was trying to save up for a boob job. I was sick of all the guys choosing me because they thought I was a very young girl; I wanted to get rid of my paedo client base. A week didn't go by without a client wanting me to put on the little-girl act for him.

I'd been thinking about having a boob job since those few nights I had worked at the stripclub. Girls there had had it done, and it seemed to have worked out all right. I didn't dare tell Layla until I had more info and, until I had the money to do it, I had all the time in the world to research and see what the options were. I had tried different make-up and clothes, and had even thought about having my hair cut, until I worked out that that would made me look even younger, but a boob job was really the only way to stop being picked as a little girl. OK, I might look young even with a boob job, but at least I would get picked by the type of guy who liked the busty look and not the guys who liked the flat-chested little-girl-lost look. Guys tended to go for a certain type, and if they didn't pick me, they'd pick Julie. If he was after one of the bustier girls, on the whole, he'd never choose Julie or I. And then there were the tall, leggy girls. They were a whole different category, and they were the ones who tended to get the more social, 'going-out' bookings, if there were any. It's true what they say: a man is either a bum, a leg or a breast man – or lack of, in my case, and I didn't like that at all.

Even though I was pale, at least I was saving. My little locked box was getting full, which was good: it wasn't just the money for the boob job I needed but also money to cover all the bills for the time I had to take off. I reckoned I needed at least £10,000 so that I could take four months off, minimum, and pay for the boob job, with a little bit spare just in case. It was more than I'd ever had to save before – my car had only been a third of what I needed now – but with the way it was going at the agency, a couple more months and I should be able to afford it – if bills didn't keep on popping up all the time.

'You know, you would do so much better if your hair were a bit lighter.' Ms Lush had said it, and so had Ms Grey, when I had my interviews, and I had heard her say it to other girls who had started after me. Agencies liked blondes – men would ask for them over the phone day in and day out – so you couldn't blame them for suggesting it: it was good business. Ms Grey had mentioned it again the other day, and I had just nodded and said, 'Maybe,' but the next time I was at the supermarket, there was a packet of bleach sitting on the shelf staring at me and, before I knew it, I had bought it. If I went blonde, maybe I would have different clients, or more, and then maybe I'd be able to afford the boob job sooner.

I didn't go totally blonde, as I panicked that I might be doing it wrong – what if it turned green? – so I washed it off too soon, and although I was now a lighter redhead, I wasn't really blonde, just more the strawberry blonde I was always sold on the phone as. I thought it still looked ginger, even if my boss didn't. The good news was that Ms Grey was pushing me harder on the phone now I was 'lighter' and I was getting more work, but the bad news was that I was still being picked by paedo clients. OK, it wasn't as if they all wanted to bounce me on their knee as such, but the creep factor was definitely there and, what was worse, they tended to be repeat clients, so they would ask for me again.

Conversation with Julie

'So, you studying?' I eyed Julie over my tea as she flicked through a huge business manual on her lap. Julie was Czech, blonde and blue-eyed, about the same height and with the same slim figure as me, and she did very well. If I had been the jealous sort, then Julie would have been my competition. Luckily, she wasn't the jealous sort either. If a guy liked her and she wasn't there, he would pick me, and vice versa. We both fell into the petite, young, girl-next-door category and, at eighteen, which was actually her real age from what I could gather, although she was quiet, Julie had her head screwed on.

She was popular with the clients, from what I could see and heard, and Ms Grey liked her too. Her English was very good, but she tended to be a girl who kept out of everyone's way and would rather read than chat, which I could fully sympathize with. Uncannily, we were fairly similar.

She looked up and shook her head. 'Not really,' she said. 'I'm saving for property back home. I reckon if I work a year here, really hard, I can buy a block of sixteen flats with a shop on the ground floor. I will turn that into a beauty salon where I can work, and I will have an apartment on the top floor.' She smiled up at me sheepishly from under her short blonde fringe.

I sat down next to her and handed her the cup of tea I had made her. 'Looks like you have it all planned out.' I took a sip of my tea as she nodded and blew on hers.

'Yes. I am not going to slave all my life washing floors and dying of exhaustion in a poky little room like my mum did.' She looked up as one of the other girls walked by and leaned closer in to me. 'You're not like them' – she looked over to Lucy, who was in the corner with a few of the older girls – 'I like you. Watch your back. They are . . . what you call it? Back-stabbing bitch,' she whispered.

I smiled faintly; I got it. Julie was basically saying that I was going to do well, and the other girls might be nice to my face, but I had better watch my back.

Mr Slimeball

Friday 6 p.m.–1 a.m.
Clients x 1 = Mr Slimeball
1 x 2 hours = £250
+ cab-fare tip = £20
Total = £270

- *agency fee £70*
- *cab fare £4 (cab back)*

Total = £196

He was sitting in the glassed-off part of the office with a notebook balanced on his knee when I was sent in to say hello.

'Please sit,' he said in a faint Italian accent, patting the chair in front of him for me to sit on. 'You a real redhead?' he queried, cocking his head to one side as he asked.

'Yes I am. Is that a problem?' I probed.

'No, not at all. I love redheads. Are you all over, collar and cuffs, as they say?' Now he was patting me on my knee. 'Ahh, nineteen, she says.' He motioned to the shadow of Ms Grey on the other side of the screen. 'I love the taste of a fresh girl.' He started to slide his hand up my skirt, at which point I stood up and smoothed it back down.

'Do you want me to send in the next girl now?'

He winked at me, got up and walked to Ms Grey's desk. 'I would like to take this beautiful girl home with me,' he said to her.

Ms Grey gestured to me and, taking her cue, I was on my way back to the girls' lounge to pick up my coat and bag while she took security info and his agency fee. He took hold of my arm as I went by and whispered in my ear, 'Take off the knickers, bella.'

He was grinning the whole time we were in the cab on the way to his house, which, considering his bad teeth, some of which were black, was slightly offputting. He spent the journey trying to stick his hand up my skirt under the prying eyes of the cabbie while in one breath talking about art and in the next how he was going to lick me out until I begged him to stop. His English was good but he still got his words a bit jumbled up. It was all I could do to stop him going down on me in the cab.

We pulled up at his very smart address and entered a wonderful apartment filled with antiques from all over the world and dotted with paintings of red-haired women, amongst all the other paintings that covered every available space there was. He offered me a drink and went off to get me some water, leaving an envelope on the side, and me to look around the room and make my security call to the agency to say I had been paid. Turning to look at a painting on the wall, I saw him standing at the door, naked, holding two glasses of water.

'Follow me, bella,' he said. 'I have a more interesting room.' And he beckoned me to follow him to his bedroom. It didn't look any more interesting to me: there were fewer things in it, mainly, a very low big bed.

Putting the glasses down on a side table, he grabbed my hand and slid his own up and down me while slobbering all over my face. I just stood there. Didn't the condemned girl at least get her drink before being jumped on?

'I take your clothes off, yes?' He nodded in answer to his own question and started undoing my dress. That would be a no then.

I just murmured yes in his ear, trying to avoid his bad breath. 'You look like one of my paintings, bella, I wanta munch your pretty pussy. Lie down, lie down.'

I lay down on the bed, and he squatted between my

legs and nuzzled my pussy. I had a dreadful feeling I was going to have to do lots of faking to keep this one happy.

'Ummm, you taste good.' The little Italian licked away and then started sucking.

I don't know what he was up to down there, but it was doing nothing for me. I looked up into his mirrored ceiling and round his opulent red-velvet-draped room and murmured as if I was enjoying myself.

'Wow, you're so wet.' He looked up, amazed, a great big grin on his face, and went back to slobbering in my pre-lubed-up crotch, mumbling away contentedly. There was no other way I was going to get wet, that was for sure. He was down there so long I was getting out of breath faking. I must have faked at least five loud orgasms by then and my time was running out, as I could see from my wristwatch. I had tried to wriggle down and get hold of his cock, but he was having none of it and clamped down in my snatch without coming up for air.

'Sit on my face. I want you to come all over it and wank me off,' he begged, lying down. I did as I was told and sat on his eager face. He came the moment I held his cock. Thank wank for that, I thought, looking at my watch again. I'd have to phone in again soon and, in addition to that, I didn't know how long I could have gone on faking without his neighbours calling the council to complain about the noise.

He got up, with dribble on his chin, looking very pleased with himself. 'I will run you a shower,' he said, and off he went down the corridor to the bathroom, while I hurried after him, picking up my bag and things as I went.

He was waiting by the front door in his long robe when I came out of his marble bathroom, dressed once more.

'Ahh, sorry, bella, I have kept you. You are such a pleasure to please. I hope you not in trouble.' He fumbled a £20 note down my front, then kissed me on the cheek as he opened the door.

'No, I called the agency and said I was on my way. If they call, just say I left ten minutes ago.'

He nodded and waved me off and I hurried down the steps, hailing a passing cab and giving the driver the name of the pub next door to the agency. Just then, my phone rang.

'Where are you?' I had called Ms Grey from the Italian's bathroom just before showering, saying I was already in a cab. I don't think she believed me, so she was calling me back to ask why I wasn't back at the office yet.

'I'm still in the cab, on my way.' I slid down the window so she could hear the traffic in the background. 'Looks like there's heavy traffic tonight,' I said, crossing my fingers and hoping I didn't get stuck in any real traffic in the ten minutes it would take to get back.

I could hear another phone ring in Ms Grey's office. She sounded distracted, saying, 'I'll call you back. Your Italian chap is on the other line.'

I sat back. The cabbie said, 'Traffic?', raising an eyebrow in the mirror at me. Nosey bugger. I laughed.

'Yes. I'm running late to meet friends – it can take a girl ages to get ready, don't you know.'

I dashed into the office. I was fifteen minutes late, but

I was hoping that traffic was a good enough excuse not to have to hand over another fee.

Ms Grey looked up. She didn't look angry. 'Your Italian called to say what a wonderful girl you are. He's booked you same time next week, for longer.' She looked very happy now.

'Oh, right.' I grinned back, hoping the disappointment didn't show on my face. I would have been quite happy to pay her another fee if it meant I hadn't had to see the slimy Italian again. I had spent far too long in the shower as it was, trying to scrub him and his garlic breath off me. I must have done too good a job faking it if he wanted me again. I don't know why he gave me the creeps, he just did.

'He has never called back for a lady before, he does the rounds of the agencies. He must really like you.' Damn, she looked pleased. I doubted I'd be able to wriggle out of double Italian next week without severe repercussions. I stomped off to the girls' lounge to boil the kettle for tea.

10. *Mr Average*

Clients × 1 = Mr Average
1 × 2 hours = £250
+ cab-fare tip = £20
Total = £270
− agency fee £70
Total = £200

You get your freaks and your regs but, on the whole, you get Mr Average. He might be the kind of client you prefer, but he is also the guy you don't remember much about. After all, what's to remember about a guy who causes you no problems and no hassle? If you have to remember details, it's usually those of the men to avoid and warn the others about. Well, I do anyhow.

Mr Average isn't really average as a person, just average Mr Nice Client. He might have some little quirk but nothing that most don't, like liking you to wear stockings. Some ask you to wear them as if it's some naughty request, as if they're asking for A levels or something. Mr Average is normally a middle-aged man in a suit, with or without glasses, maybe with a bald spot just appearing on the horizon, with a bit of a paunch and/or love handles from working too hard at his desk; he doesn't have time for the gym. Medium height, dark hair, works in IT, a bank or has his own company. He's been married a couple of years and the wife, after having a kid or two, has gone off sex. Even the nicest man finds it hard if they haven't had sex in a year, and then he'll wander. I had one who had waited twelve years to get his leg over, but the average was around two years. By then they were wound so tight a smaller head had starting to do their thinking for them. Mr Average still loves his wife but that doesn't stop him having the normal male urges and, rather than having an affair, he turns to the less complicated option – a working girl who's there for his needs and gives him confidence, proving he hasn't lost it.

Mr Average is a nice guy, normally, grateful and no hassle. All the girls tend to like Mr Average. The only problem is that he can be so starved of affection, his wife's having gone from him to his kids, or so he thinks, you have to be careful he doesn't start to believe he's in love with you.

There are so many men with the same MO that, after a while, you tend not to notice much about them, other than remembering which hotel it is and the right room number. In fact, as you see the same type of guy all the time, and Mr Average is easy to forget, he ends up pretty much being just a room number. Mr Favourite Regular Client might be a Mr Average too, but Mr Fave Reg is more memorable; there are some men you just click with, in terms of humour and chemistry. For some strange reason, I always seem to have three Mr Fave Regs at any one time – no, not some orgy!; three men I see separately who I get on really well with. Maybe every now and then one will leave to work abroad, or his wife will get back on track and be putting out again, so they might never call for me again, but they are soon replaced by a new favourite. Some just push my buttons more than normal, but I am a sucker for a gift – what girl isn't? – especially something I've really wanted, like a new book I've been trying to get hold of. A gift doesn't have to be expensive, if it's thoughtful, but every little helps.

Where was I? Oh, yes – a date with Mr Average. A call comes through (Mr Average tends to call rather than come in), then I flag down a black cab outside and go to a nice four-star hotel within the Triangle. The Triangle is a bit like the Bermuda Triangle but, in London, it's the area the agencies consider there to be the greatest concentration of the richest pockets, where money easily leaves men's wallets, leaving them with nothing but a happy smile on their face. It stretches from Marylebone to West Kensington, then down to Chelsea and back up. Most of the top hotels and expensive houses are in the Triangle. Other than that, there's the occasional airport booking. To begin with, I thought that, with the City being the big financial centre in London, we would get more calls from that area. After all, at the sauna, a lot of the men who came in had come in from the City, for a cheap quickie in their lunchbreak. But I soon realized that, as an escort, you were in a whole different league. The men I saw now were more interested in spending £200 for a relaxed two-hour evening booking in a nice hotel than £80 for a half-hour fuck on an uncomfortable massage table. Not that there wasn't money in the City, but if a gent had money to spend on an 'upmarket girl', as they called us, he tended to stay in one of the nice hotels in the Triangle. The City didn't really have any nice big hotels to speak of back then. £200 was pretty much average for an agency – you couldn't really hire an escort in London for less than £180 – but there were agencies that charged up to £300 for two hours. The more they charged, the harder they were to work for; you needed to be recommended or know someone even to get an interview. £200 was still a lot of money, and not something the average working man would be willing to pay, so our Mr Average client normally had a good job, not just an average one.

So, back to the date with Mr Average. I turn up at the hotel and walk in briskly, looking like I know where I am going, and walk confidently but not in too much of a hurry towards the lifts. There is nothing that alerts nosey hotel staff more than someone walking into a lobby late at night, alone, dressed up to the nines and looking around like she doesn't know where she's going. If it's a hotel you haven't been to before, at least one of the girls will generally know whereabouts the lift is in the lobby, so it's worth asking before you leave the agency. The girls even played a game when they were waiting in the lounge between clients. In 'Where The Lifts Are', you have to give directions, such as 'past the reception desk on your right, round the corner, under the arch,' and say whether a card key is needed to operate the lift; even a scribbled diagram is helpful sometimes. If there is a card-key system for the lift, you have to ask the agency to phone the client and have him meet you in the lobby. But, with most, you could just take the stairs and bypass the system that way. Not many hotels do have card-key locks on the lifts – and thank goodness, as it's hard enough trying to enter a hotel discreetly and not give your client away as it is. Not that the hotel could do much about it, but there is always the chance that some snooty bellboy could give you hassle and ask, with a raised eyebrow and a downward look, if he can help you.

Getting to the right hotel door and making a quick note of the time (if I was more than five minutes early, I would hide out in the hotel lobby's toilet), I take a deep breath to calm my nerves and put a big smile on my face to calm his, then knock lightly on the door. I quickly unbutton my long coat, as showing a bit of cleavage and some leg as he opens the door never goes amiss – first impressions and all that.

'Hello, John?' I give the client a hug or a peck on the cheek so I can look over his shoulder; he nods and ushers me into the room, after putting the do-not-disturb sign on the door. I take a quick look around the room to make sure he's on his own and that the room looks safe, keeping my back to the entrance wall as I slide my coat off and let my keys, which I keep gripped in my hand as a form of self-defence weapon, slip back into the pocket, then hand my coat to him when he offers to hang it up. 'Thank you. So, do you have a view?' I ask, even if it's obvious that he doesn't, just because it gives me a chance to cross the room and him to have a good look at me, top to toe. I lean over the windowsill so my stocking tops just show under my tight, short but not too short, dress – that has Mr Average in a good mood from the get-go.

The client usually offers me a drink (I always ask for water) and I find a chair or somewhere to perch where I can see him pouring it. I only ever pretend to drink it, just in case he has slipped something into it.

I ask something along the lines of, 'So, you here on business?', something inoffensive so no uncomfortable silence follows, and then keep chatting away to make the client feel at ease. If after ten minutes or so (I always keep an eye on my watch) he hasn't mentioned or brought out an envelope, I ask, 'So would you like me to stay?', which has Mr Average nodding, 'Oh yes,' and fumbling around for the money, looking rather embarrassed that he hadn't thought of it sooner or hadn't known how to bring it up. If he needs more prompting, I use the 'I have to call the agency as a safety check and let them know you've paid' line.

By this time, I've made sure that my skirt has risen up as I sit, and lean forward so that what little cleavage I have is on view to Mr Average, who generally just looks a bit dense, or else shy and distracted. Next I pick up my bag and motion towards the loo, and the client nods again, and I dial the agency to check in. I close the bathroom door behind me and let the agency know I've been paid, quickly counting out the money. It just doesn't feel right counting it out in front of him. Putting it in the side pocket of my bag, I pick out a standard-sized condom and secure it in the top of my stocking ready for use, then liberally apply some lube, wash my hands and fish my massage gel out of my bag. Meanwhile, Mr Average has been waiting nervously in the room, all sorts of thoughts running through his head about what is going to happen next.

I know what's going to happen next, so I'm not at all nervous. I know I will start by unbuttoning his shirt and undressing him, making him lie face down on the bed and giving him a massage for around fifteen minutes as he is bound to be a bit stressed. I wrestle his novelty boxer shorts off, saying he doesn't need them. He's all too eager and helps me push them down his legs and off the end of the bed.

Mr Average is always a bit anxious: his wife and kids make him stressed, work makes him frazzled, the gym makes him tense and, on top of it all, waiting for some unknown girl to turn up at his hotel door has made him nervy. At this point, around forty-five minutes has passed since I entered the hotel room, and Mr Average is relaxed as I have massaged him from head to foot and back up again, a full-on proper massage, not too hard unless he asks me – none of this namby-pamby business just pushing oil around his back that clients tell me they sometimes get from other girls. From all my hours of experience at the massage parlour and the brothel, I'm bound to give good hand – I learned from some of the best, after all.

The massage is to get Mr Average's blood flowing and to relax him, but by now, with a nearly nude girl at his side rubbing him all over, he has started to get uncomfortable lying on his now prominent erection. If it's not yet prominent, it will be at least semi-hard, and the next stage will have him ready for me. I whip off my bra and, now topless, I finish the massage. He turns over to see why I have stopped and is faced with breasts and prominent nipples (I pinch them to make them look perky when I take off my bra). He eyes me, looks up politely and asks, 'Can I?', meaning can he touch and suck, to which the answer is 'Yes, I love that.'

I stroke up and down his leg, not quite touching his cock, as he sucks and fumbles at my breasts. I suck in my breath and enjoy the feeling of his hands travelling over my body and we roll over on the bed. When he starts to travel further down I push him back a little and kiss downwards from his chest, reaching for the condom in my stockings and checking out his cock so that I can be sure the condom will fit. (If not I dive over the bed and rescue another from my bag.) Mr Average is propping himself up, looking down at me as I roll on the rubber and suck him. I look up into his eyes and, if he wasn't hard before, he is certainly getting that way now as I play with his balls and carry on sucking, making sure that I don't carry on for too long and make him come before we have sex. He might feel cheated, especially as I still have my knickers on.

Facing him, I inch my thong down my legs, still sucking and stopping only to completely remove my thong and squat over his cock ready to slide slowly down it, gripping all the way, so that even if he has a smallish cock he feels every inch. Mr Average watches, holding his breath as I clench tight and push down slowly to draw his cock in. It's now around an hour and a quarter since I entered the room. I don't even have to look at my watch, as I can see the clock in the phone by the bed. If we have sex any sooner, I know we'll be finished too early and he might not feel he's had his money's worth and might not book me again, and repeat customers are what I am aiming for. You know what you're getting with a repeat client, and a Mr Average is one you want to come again and again.

If he's dragging it out, and moving on to missionary hasn't worked because he's trying not to come then doggie-style normally does the trick. If poor Mr Average hasn't popped by then, it's down to the fact that he hasn't had sex in a while and is out of practice. The last resort and a big hint that he should come soon is asking, 'Where would you like to come, what about over my tits?' After that, a lubed hand job over my chest will finish him off and have me dashing off to the bathroom for tissues to wipe us off with. If there is still time, I'll sit, chat and fetch Mr Average his drink or some water before I retreat to the bathroom with my things to wash, shower and re-do my make-up and hair.

I'll be ready to leave then and give Mr Average a peck on the cheek and a wave. He'll be wearing a robe and will pretty much automatically slip a £20 note for cab fare into my hand (the agency would have said on the phone that I would need cab fare to get to him and back, or he would have seen another girl in the past and know the score – even if he claims he hasn't out of some strange sort of desire to spare your feelings). You rarely have to ask Mr Average for cab fare, and even if you do, he's happy to give it, now having a huge grin on his face.

And that's about it for a Mr Average booking – all very convenient for me: some sex, some money and I'm on my way. The door closes on Mr Average, and I go back to the agency, fingers crossed to pick up another that I would have some fun with and forget just as easily.

Mr Paedo Pilot

Monday 3 p.m.– 1 a.m.

Clients x 1 = Mr Paedo Pilot

1 x 2 hours = £250

+ cab-fare tip = £40

Total = £290

– agency fee £70

– cab fare £8 (cab back)

Total = £212

He looked very smart but was a bit on the quiet side but, saying that, most gents who came in were a bit intimidated by the surroundings so that wasn't surprising. Ms Grey had popped her head around the door after the buzzer went and asked that only Julie and I come out and say hello. There were other girls the same age as we were supposed to be in the lounge, so the fact that she had just asked young, blonde Julie and skinny me had Julie rolling her eyes at me across the room. We both knew it meant that the man who had come in had asked for a younger girl.

Julie went first. 'I've seen him before,' she whispered ominously when she came back into the lounge. 'He'll want you this time.'

I walked out and said hello to the chap. He was in his early thirties and was dressed in a smart suit, and had dark hair and a neat moustache, which made him look rather distinguished. He smiled, said a brief hello, then stood and turned to Ms Grey, getting out his wallet to pay her the introduction fee, which I took as my cue to go and get my coat and bag. I had pulled.

Julie was waiting at the door when I came back into the lounge. 'OK, what's he into then?' I asked, going over to pick up my bag. One of the girls shushed me, as the other girls were watching the end of some soap on the TV.

'He's OK. Quick booking, just likes a fumble and a feel under the covers. Likes you to lie there and not do or say much. No groaning – he told me to stop last time.' I patted her shoulder and mouthed thanks, even so earning another 'Sssssh' from one of the girls. With that advice from Julie, I pulled on my coat and headed out of the door with my client to catch a cab back to his apartment, which was some distance away, in a posh area. We chatted a bit in the cab and I found out that he was a pilot, or so he said, and he proceeded to talk about flying. He seemed very normal.

It wasn't until after I had taken the money he gave me and phoned in for the so-called security check that his manner changed from quietly confident to just plain quiet. I had just sat down. He had offered me a drink and was just off to the open-plan kitchen I could see around the corner when he asked me to go into the bedroom across the hall and wait for him there.

'Can you take everything off, put on the underwear laid on the bed and slide under the covers for me?' He used a creepy, low-pitched tone which, if Julie hadn't had words with me before I left, would probably have had me freaking out. Getting up and walking into the bedroom, I could have guessed that the underwear was going to be a big white pair of cotton panties. I had changed and was just lying there under the covers as he had asked when he came in and gave me a glass of water. I thanked him and asked him to put it down on the side table. He started to climb in on the other side of the bed fully clothed, but I heard his zipper as he reached to turn the side lights down so that we were lying in the gloom and quiet. He obviously didn't want to talk much. He just whispered, 'Daddy just wants you to lie there . . . sssh, there's a good girl.'

My skin was crawling. I just lay there and thought about other things: in a couple of months' time he wouldn't even think of picking me; just a few months and I wouldn't have this type of client. I crossed my fingers as he stroked my crotch in the white cotton knickers. He didn't say very much after that and, after what Julie had said, I didn't so much as moan. I could tell he didn't want me to anyhow. From what I could see from the move-ment under the covers, he was wanking himself off with one hand while stroking the white cotton with the other. It only lasted a few minutes, then he gave a little sigh, came under the covers and stopped stroking.

I looked over at him. There was just his head sticking out from the covers and he was still an arm's length away. He looked happy enough. 'There's a good girl. You can go in the bathroom now and get dressed,' he said, nod-ding to the adjoining bathroom. Taking the things I had piled on top of my bag at the side of the bed, I slid the condom I was still holding back into the side pocket without him seeing. He was sitting up now, facing away, as I headed to the bathroom to get washed and dressed. I left the cotton panties on the laundry basket there –

it wasn't like I wanted them: I hadn't worn anything like that since middle school. I didn't take long getting dressed again – my make-up and hair were still fine – and I walked out to find him dressed in a robe and sitting in the lounge as if nothing had happened.

'I'll call you a cab, they're hard to find around here.' Gone was his creepy, quiet voice and back was the confident man who had chatted away earlier about flying. I don't know what I expected, but it was all very strange: most men at least wanted sex, especially the guys who wanted you to act young. I was sent on my way with a £40 tip after some small talk about the weather and was back at the agency within an hour of leaving it. The money was good, but I would have preferred to have normal sex rather than all the creepiness and no sex any day. Getting paid for not having sex is never as easy as it sounds – there is always some nasty catch.

I hoped that this particular nasty catch would pick a different girl next time, like he had after seeing Julie before me. Seeing paedo clients was all very profitable, but it wasn't getting any easier. If I could change my main client base, I'd be so much happier. Maybe if I saw more of the nicer clients I got every now and then, my anxiety attacks – if that's what my paranoid bad moods were – would stop. I did get them more when I had seen a paedo client. The bigger, bustier girls didn't have the problem of being cooed over or bounced on some pseudo-grandfather's knee. If it was going to take a boob job to escape that type of client it would be worth the ten months' solid working and saving I had calculated it would take. It was time to do some more research, interrogate some doctors and surgeons, and talk to some other girls who had had it done. Who says you have to lie back and think of England? I was going to lie back and think of Enlargement.

11. *Spank You Very Much: Fetish Clubs*

Samantha had come into the agency the week before waving a flier for a fetish club she wanted to go to. She was looking for girls to go with her, as she had never been to one before and thought it might be a laugh. Intrigued as I was, I didn't think it was a good idea to go with her: Samantha was a complete space cadet and she got into trouble at normal clubs, being thrown out because she was legless. I had heard the other girls gossiping about it in the lounge. Samantha was a party girl, but one that was forever landing herself in the shit, so I wasn't surprised no one wanted to tag along with her. I'd never been to a fetish club before either and, bar a few clients who had mentioned having been, I don't think I even knew anyone who had. I didn't want to end up in some dark place somewhere with my back up against a wall and no one I could trust to bail me out if everything went whip-shaped. But that didn't mean that I didn't want to go and check one out some time. Layla would be a perfect choice to drag along with me: she was ever so slightly kinky and was always game for a laugh. I'd ask her when she next came to stay for a weekend in London as a break from uni.

Well, that weekend had arrived, and here we were. The fetish night was being held in some dark tunnels underneath some railway arches, and it was all a bit of a maze. I had already lost Layla – one minute she was by my side and the next she had wandered off. Neither of us had known what to expect but, apart from the fact that the crowd was dressed differently, it was pretty much like a normal nightclub but with a bit of kinkiness thrown in and some leather benches and metal-framed contraptions in various corners. I spotted Layla – she hadn't wandered far: I could see her on the other side of the tunnel, chatting up some bloke dressed from top to toe in leather and with rather large spikes on his shoulders.

'Go on, spank me, please. I want to feel what it's like.' A girl of Amazonian build looked up at me with big, pleading eyes from where she was seated. Layla and I had sparked up a conversation earlier in the toilets with some very friendly rubber-clad girls, who had been tottering around on their heels, faffing in front of the mirrors. And for the past hour we had all been chatting, sitting round the bar and people-watching. It was Miss Amazon's first time at the club; her friends had brought her. The girls' dresses were brand-new and shiny, and made them look very fetish indeed. Layla was in a black sari with elaborate glitter make-up and long eyelashes and I was wearing a red-satin corset top, a lace-up thong I had made, red fishnet tights and a pair of shiny red platform boots I'd found in Camden. The other week Layla and I had gone looking for a fetish dress shop there. It had moved premises and we hadn't been able to find it, so we had had to make do – and from the wide range of looks and styles sported by the eclectic crowd, it looked like we had done the right thing. The rubber girls assumed we had been lots of times before; I think we looked as if we belonged.

Some guy had come in bare-chested, wearing black jeans, and a matronly-looking, larger lady in an over-tight PVC dress made a comment to me about him at the bar when I went for drinks. She said he shouldn't have been allowed in, that he stood out like a sore thumb and hadn't made any effort at all. If he didn't have the imagination and creativity to be bothered to dress appropriately, he had to be a really bad shag. I nodded to her and made my escape. She carried on making over-loud comments in his direction, and the people around her started giving the guy dirty looks, until he shuffled off, not knowing what he had done that was so wrong. It seemed that fetish clubs had more rules than I had realized. And it wasn't just the rules on the tickets or the signs in the entrance of a normal club about dress code here; the way you dressed gave a statement about your sexual persuasion. Devil only knew what signals my outfit was giving off then! But whatever statement it was making, it was obviously working. Not a single man had pinched my bum, and all the people who had approached me had been very respectful and polite. From what I had seen, no one grabbed; they always asked first. A leather-masked gimp had been following me around, and I hadn't been able to get rid of him, much to Layla's amusement, and in the end I had told him to bugger off, only to have him bow and apologize, saying, oddly, 'Thank you very much.' Then he just disappeared into the crowd – no getting the hump or all pissy as some men did in normal nightclubs.

There was only a smattering of people wearing rubber, and the four girls we were with were having a few problems with it. It was all new to them – they all had identical-looking black, shiny rubber on, no personal touches – and being on 'a novel naughty night out', as one of them put it, they had not known to powder the inside of their dresses and were now sitting stickily on their stools. Two of the girls were also complaining about aching feet, as they were also wearing new shoes and looked rather uncomfortable in them. Miss Amazon was the only one who looked like she was enjoying the sensation of the rubber.

We had just been treated to a display by a lad wearing only a thong. He was bending over one of the stools next to us and had asked one of the rubber girls to spank him with his leather paddle. She giggled and happily obliged him, giving him ten of the best on his bare bum, teetering on her very high new heels as she did so. Then he dropped his white hankie, which was a substitute for his safety word to let her know to stop. The club was loud, and he might not be heard, he said. He looked very pleased with himself and knelt at her feet, licking her shoes in thanks, much to the girl's mirth. She was still holding his paddle.

What little I knew of fetishes had been passed on from other girls I had worked with, and particularly Bella, a brothel dom I had known in the past. The spanking was obviously a real novelty to the rubber girls, as they couldn't stop tittering, but it wasn't that foreign to me. Having said that, it wasn't something that featured in your normal Saturday night out either, that was for sure, and neither were the setting or the crowd of strangely dressed people.

As the night progressed, people had become more confident. Layla and I watched, nonplussed, on the sidelines.

Layla had corrected the rubber-girl spanker so she was spanking upward with the small leather paddle rather than down, as she had a very heavy hand – either that or she was more tipsy by then than we realized.

'Go on, please spank me, too,' said Miss Amazon, eyeing up the submissive's leather paddle and hankie, which were now lying on the table, abandoned in his pursuit of shoes to lick. The man in the leather gear had come back to chat to Layla, and she passed me the spanking paddle with a wink and stood back to make some room.

'Are you sure?' *I* wasn't at all sure – I might have gently hand-spanked a naughty client before, but I'd never paddled a girl. But, if the other girl could do it and it was her first time too, then so could I. Miss Amazon rolled up her rubber dress until it was around her waist and bent over her stool, hankie in hand and her pink thong showing off a pert bottom. It wasn't surprising that a crowd gathered around: Miss Amazon's bottom was far cuter than that of the skinny submissive. I pulled back and gave her a genteel whack to start with.

I bent over her. 'How's that?' I queried.

'Harder,' came the reply, with a big grin.

Well, she asked for it. I flexed my shoulders, turned sideways on and stood my ground, making sure I had a clear space to pull back my hand. I spanked her harder and she wiggled, so I took a step back for more leverage and hit her harder again. This time a small red line was etched across her left buttock. She stopped wiggling but did not drop the hankie, so I changed hands and evened things out by giving her a whack on the right cheek as well.

It was a bit strange dealing out pain when I generally dealt in pleasure, but she seemed to be enjoying it, because she wiggled to be hit again. I know people can be strange but, to me, pain hurts, it's not pleasurable at all, yet here were people who were enjoying and feeling pleasure in the release of endorphins. I might not get it, but if the pain was pleasurable to them, then dishing it out made me feel good, in a weird sort of way. I hit her harder but consistently. Even so it lasted longer, but she took it, egged on by the crowd, who were enjoying the spectacle. She screamed and panted as her rosy bottom became an even red all over. I couldn't help but think it was a very unusual canvas to lay my mark on, wondering about the way the colour changed, how red it would get, and how long it would last once I'd stopped.

I eased off on the spanking, and stroked her sensitive cheeks with my nails and blew on her flesh. That made her shudder, it was so unexpected – and pinging the elastic of her thong was unexpected, too, as I eased back, kicking her feet further apart, ready to continue adding to the hue on her gleaming rear. Her knees shook.

Unfortunately, white-hankie boy was now pissing me off. He was in the way, and as I stood back I accidentally trod on his hand. I was sure he'd put it there on purpose, because he grinned up at me.

'Oh, go and make yourself useful. Get me a glassful of ice,' I said, rousing him to his feet and pushing him towards the bar and out of my way. I stretched back to give a very hard pelt to the girl's bottom, which was still wiggling and now glowing. I gave her three more slow, very hard strokes of the leather hand paddle, putting all my strength into it and trying not to slide back on the floor in my heels from the forward force, before she whimpered, dropped the hankie and stood, rubbing her hands over her rear. Hankie Boy had been lurking by my side for the last stroke, holding a pint glass full of ice as if it were some sort of trophy. I took it from his hands, ignoring his look of confusion. 'It's not for you,' I said, turning to put a reassuring hand on Miss Amazon's back. 'Bend back over and stay still,' I said, and she complied with another shudder. I slowly placed a cold hand on her pink cheeks and started rubbing ice cubes along the flesh, as Hankie Boy knelt at my side, having reclaimed the glass of ice and holding it for me.

It had all become clear to him now, and he beamed up, a contented lapdog at my feet. An all-too-pleading look of 'Me next' was written all over his face, but I shooed him off to take the glass back to the bar, handing him his paddle and telling him that if he came back in an hour and found me I might spank him too. The girls giggled, and Miss Amazon looked pleased, showing off her red bum to anyone and everyone who passed. Layla was finding it all very amusing.

An hour later, Hankie Boy came back to pester me. I sat and made him lick my boots and let Layla deal with him, and she administered the paddle, much to his delight. Afterwards, we slipped into the crowd, losing Hankie Boy, who was becoming a bit clingy. The rubber girls and Miss Amazon, her dress still hitched up around her waist (she couldn't roll it down or sit), had tottered off to the dance floor. We left before the end so we wouldn't have to wait around in the queue for our bags and long coats.

Recalling the events of that night in the car on our way back to the flat, Layla and I agreed that we'd go again when we next had a chance – and when we had found something else to wear. As far as I was concerned, dressing up to go was just as much fun as being there.

Mr Panic

Thursday 6 p.m.–1 a.m.
Clients x 1 = Mr Panic
1 x 2 hours = £250
Cab-fare tip = £0
Total = £250
– agency fee £70
– cab fare £6 (cab back)
Total = £174

When we said hello in the introduction booth, we weren't really allowed to talk about any sexual act. In the office, Ms Grey was adamant that nothing was discussed; we were selling our time, not sex – but it did make it a bit difficult for the client. It didn't stop some of them from asking all sorts of things, though. If they did, we weren't supposed to say yes but were meant to infer that it was acceptable. 'I think we will have a lot of fun' or 'I might be the girl for you' with a wink normally worked. If the client was being particularly dense and kept on asking sexual questions, a whispered 'I'm sorry but we can't speak about that' stopped him. Men who came in through the door knew the score – the agency had been there for years and most of them had been before – and walk-ins who had never been to an escort agency before were rare. There were pretty much two types of agency: sit-in, like the one I was working in, and a few old-fashioned photo-album agencies, where clients went to an office and picked a girl from a photo and description and she was sent to him. Samantha said she had worked for one but liked sit-in better as it meant she worked set times and didn't have to wait at home dressed up and always ready to go whenever she was called for.

Anyway, as soon as this particular guy came in we had a feeling he was a new walk-in. The routine was that we would all go out one at a time to say a brief hello and then the client would pick a few girls to have a quick chat with in the introduction area before he made his choice – but this gent tried to ask the first girl who went in a few questions.

'Think we have a new one out there,' said Julie. She had been the first one to go out and say hello. Ms Grey had seated him in the glassed-off area and we all went in separately for a chat. The girl before me came back into the lounge shaking her head in my direction. 'You're up next,' she said. She kicked off her shoes and sat down. 'He's not a gentleman, that one – asked if he could fuck me here!' She looked shocked and repulsed. She was

174

fairly new, and I guess she'd never really worked before, or at another agency.

I smiled at her and patted her knee as I passed on my way out. 'Fancy him asking that!'

'So, do you suck without?' I had just sat down, and that was the first thing he had asked me. He looked really nervous, sitting there in his smart, pinstriped suit.

'Er no,' I said, getting up from my seat to leave. 'I don't think I am the girl for you.' So much for that. Pity – he smelled of money, from the expensive Italian shoes to the real-gold watch on his wrist. A girl tends to notice fast what a client wears.

'No, I think you are.' He stood too. 'I don't want a girl who does.'

'What?' I was puzzled. 'Then why ask?'

He smiled, sitting down again and gesturing for me to do the same. I stayed standing, raising my eyebrows, still wondering what he was going on about.

'I want a . . .' he looked a bit stuck for words '. . . a safe girl for a few hours, not one that takes risks.' I had a feeling the new girl before me had given him the 'We can't talk about that' line, so now he was finding it difficult. 'Sorry. I haven't done this before,' he said, looking up at me.

I must have smiled, because he started to look less nervous. 'I think I probably am the girl for you, but do you want me to send in the last two ladies to say hello?'

'Do you have to?' He stood up and looked around as I started to leave. He had jumped up so fast it was like musical chairs.

I turned to reassure him that, no, I didn't have to but it might be best to at least see them. 'Don't want them getting jealous of me, now do we?' I winked. 'You can always ask the lady at the desk for Susan – that's me – afterwards . . . if you haven't changed your mind?'

'Susan. Right, got it. Susan,' he muttered as I left to send in the next girl.

Either the other girls didn't take his fancy or they had answered his questions wrongly but Ms Grey popped her head around the lounge door and told me I'd been picked and to go and grab my stuff while she dealt with the agency fee and the security information of the hotel I was going to.

All the way to the hotel in the cab he hardly said a thing he was so jittery. He was a bit more relaxed back at his hotel room, but even so . . .

I should have named him Mr Bad Shag. He pushed in, pulled all the way out, pushed in again and then all the way out again quickly. He went on and on, doing the same thing. I could feel him pumping me full of air, and it wasn't pleasant. Any moment now and he would be causing a fanny fart. I tried turning sideways, which wasn't easy, as I was bent over the bed. It relieved the pressure a bit, but the thrusting and stabbing with his hard cock was getting a bit painful. Luckily, he came, with a grunt, in no time at all, and spread out, a spent force, over me. He was an OK guy; shame about the bad sex. There wasn't much I could have done about it, though: I had asked him to take it slower and tried different positions, but to no effect; he just kept on drawing all the way out and ramming all the way in again no matter what. If that was the way he went at it with his wife, I wasn't surprised she was refusing to have sex with him, or so he said. I didn't even want to think about what his kissing technique might be. Like most clients, he didn't even try to kiss me. I probably would have chipped a tooth if the sex had been anything to go by.

'OK, I'm done' was all he said as he pulled away, not even looking at me. He went into the bathroom to shower. I sat up and gathered my things, ready to pop into the shower after him. He was in the bathroom for what seemed an age. What was he up to? I thought it was supposed to be women who spent ages in the bathroom? A glance at my cheap watch told me that he had spent longer in the bathroom than he had in me!

I re-did my make-up while I waited, sitting on the side of the bed, and then straightened the bedclothes and spread out his discarded clothing on top. He came out wrapped in his robe, smelling of soap and looking rather pleased with himself.

'All yours.' Mr Panic motioned to the still-running, steaming shower through the open doorway as he made his way to the mini-bar to fix himself a drink. I hunted for a shower cap in my bag, got off the bed and headed towards the steam. I had a quick shower, managing not to disturb my make-up, dried off and dressed ready to leave.

He was grinning as he walked me to the door, shook my hand and proposed a longer booking, with dinner, when he was back in town in two weeks' time. I said he should call the agency and started to hand him a card, but he fended it off. Didn't want the wife to find it, so he said.

He waved me off on my way to catch a cab back to the agency without having given me the usual cab-fare tip. I still hadn't worked out a good way of asking for it without feeling as if it sounded cheeky, especially as he had just handed me what I saw as a lot of money, in comparison to what I had earned in the past. I'd ask Layla – she'd know how to do it nicely without getting the client's back up.

Knickers in a Twist

How do you get your knickers off? Now, you would think that, for a whore, it would be an easy business – a whore's drawers are always hitting the floor, right? Well, not really – especially if they are expensive, pretty ones. You don't want to go throwing those on a patch of baby oil and spoiling the fabric or toss them willy-nilly at some naked tea light and scorch an unsought-after crotchless effect in them, not if they have cost you a shag to buy them. (Hands up anyone who has done either of those two things. OK. That'll just be me then.) Well, back to the problem of getting my knickers out of a twist.

Picture the scene. You're giving a guy a massage, and he has wandering hands, so you leave your knickers on till the last possible point so he won't ram his thick and grimy-nailed fingers, which have been goodness only knows where, up you. Keeping your knickers on means that he can't get that far; they stand guard until you can get in position, ready to sit on his, hopefully, hard cock. You know that, at this point, if you take your hand away for a second or two, you can shuffle your knickers off down your legs, over your shoes if you haven't already taken them off or if he's asked you to keep them on. But maybe you've tumbled around, and he's rubbered up, and you're in some daft position you don't even know how you got into, because he's got an image in his head of some Kama Sutra porno he was watching before you arrived, and you don't know he's been watching it let alone have any idea of the plot ... And then, to have the moment spoilt because you still have those pesky difficult-to-get-out-of-in-a-horizontal-position knickers on. By the time you get back to the cock ready to do the business, it's been and gone all floppy on you.

When I worked in the sauna, I had noticed that Zora had some knickers with a side fastening. They were a cheap, stripper's pair and looked like bikini briefs. They only unfastened on one side, but she said they did the trick in terms of easy, quick removal if you were straddling some chap who had a yo-yo-dick problem. She said they were really useful, but she had bought them in Australia and hadn't been able to find them in England. You could buy silk side-tie ones in the really expensive shops, but they cost far too much for me in those days for just a work thong – not that I had found any shops that sold such a thing anyway. My only option was to add side ribbons, poppers or a hook to pairs of knickers I already had. That should solve the problem.

Or that's what I thought. But ribbons and side ties are all very well, but getting them caught on a guy's watch doesn't help the mood; they are fiddly and difficult to tie straight; and they give your outline a weird lump on the hips through your clothes. Poppers kept coming undone every time I sat down – providing no end of amusement for the girls one afternoon when I stood up and my thong un-popped and slid down my legs on to the floor. So they were out.

In the end, the only thing that worked was a hook-and-eye fastening on each side. The hook had to face out, as I painfully found out. I'm not surprised people say that whores wear no drawers! It would be a damn sight easier than spending a great many evenings taking apart perfectly good pairs of knickers to sew on fiddly hooks and eyes.

12. *A Miss is as Good as a Mister*

'She's going on about how much she likes anal,' whispered Samantha, who was earwigging at the lounge door, listening in to a girl who had come in late for an interview. 'She's going on and on about it. She sounds Brazilian, wants to do strap-on too.' Samantha flopped down on to the chair next to me.

'I heard Brazilians are like that,' piped up Lucy, sounding all smug. Which, coming from her, was a bit rich, as we all knew it was she who was sent when a client asked for anything back door.

'Afraid she'll take all your business then, are we?' Samantha countered, and Lucy huffed and stomped off to the kitchenette.

'Helloo, girls.' A dark-skinned Brazilian lady dressed in bright colours bounded in through the doorway.

'The Mzzz said I should look around.' She sat down on one of the spare couches, crossing her long legs and tossing her hair extensions back over her shoulder. 'So is this it, sit-in? Just a dark lounge?'

She was very friendly and I couldn't help but smile. 'No, there's a loo and kitchenette over there.' I pointed to the corner.

'Aren't you adorable! So tiny!' She beamed at me. I didn't know if it was meant as a compliment or not, but I took it as one.

'I am now Gina.' She proffered her hand to Samantha and me, and both of us shook it. The only other escort in the room was sliding lower down behind her newspaper in her seat to avoid having to shake hands with our new comrade in charms. 'It's *very* dark in here.'

Gina looked around, and Samantha bombarded her with questions. Samantha always wanted to know everything. Learning about people was better than watching the soaps on the TV, she said. I had taken to Gina, and not just because she was so different to me that there was no way she was going to attract the same gents as I would, but because at least she was cheerful. She looked as if she was a naturally merry sort, unlike Samantha, who was bouncy because of her 'slimming tablets' (code for speed, really), and it lightened the mood and made the nights sitting around in the lounge pass more quickly if there was a cheerful girl around.

Lucy had been lurking in the background holding a cup of tea and came over to say a too-bright hello. Samantha had now run out of questions about the agency in Brazil Gina had last worked at.

It wasn't until Gina was called to the office by Ms Grey to sign her contract to start work that night that Lucy sidled over to me whispering, 'She's a he, I swear.'

'Don't be daft, she's stunning,' said an indignant Samantha.

'She looked like a girl to me! She can't be a man – I couldn't see an Adam's apple,' I hissed back at Lucy.

'You're just jealous. She's Brazilian – of course she's a bit dramatic, with all that Latin-American blood.' Samantha wasn't going to be budged.

'I'm telling you: she's a chick with a dick. I've seen it before.' Lucy crossed her arms.

'She's a man,' piped up the other escort there, who was still hiding behind her broadsheet.

'Well, then, you have nothing to worry about then, do you?' Samantha got up to go and listen at the door again.

Lucy turned to me. 'She still on speed, or is it coke now?' She motioned to Samantha, who was chewing a nail, tapping her foot and fidgeting, her ear to the door of the next room.

I just shrugged and picked up my book.

'Oh, fuck, she's sending her to see Bad John.' Samantha grimaced. 'Got to warn her what he's like.'

'She'll be fine,' grinned Lucy. 'Might even give him what he's asking for.'

'Shit, she's going straight there. Didn't she have a coat to come back and get?' Samantha pushed away from the door frame to pace the room, looking about her.

'No,' both Lucy and I said, almost simultaneously.

'She kept it on, Sam. Will you sit down? You're making me nervous.' I patted the seat next to me.

Gina was back before long. When the door buzzer went we started getting ready, putting on our shoes and re-doing our lipgloss, thinking that it was a client. She didn't know that we all buzzed three times so everyone knew it was a girl coming back and not a client and didn't have to bother getting up and ready. As we were now all assembled near the door, we couldn't miss hearing the conversation in the office.

'He is a nasty pig . . . I even suck him off, he kick me

out and he no pay me.' Gina sounded really pissed off. The phone rang and Ms Grey picked it up and began murmuring to someone else on the other end. Over the top of the conversation, Gina was demanding, 'Now you pay me. You sent me, and he have no idea how to treat a lady.'

'Yes, but you're not even a lady,' Ms Grey sneered back, just after we heard the click of the receiver being put down in the office. It must have been Bad John on the other end, telling his sordid side of the story, as he always did after Ms Grey sent him a new girl.

'In Brazil that don't matter. I am more of a lady than any of your sheep escorts in there.' Gina was sounding really loud and nasty now. 'You pay me for the cock I sucked now,' she demanded again, this time with a *thump*, which I guessed was her hand hitting the office desk.

'I don't think so, mister. Now, get out, you liar, and don't come back.' Now it was Ms Grey's voice that was drowning out Gina's. For such a small, frail-looking lady, she had a very powerful voice – it could stop phone masturbators at a stroke – and at that volume, even in the next room I was scared of her.

'See!' Lucy looked so very smug. 'I think the boss might need a hand,' she said, rushing to the aid of Ms Grey. From the sound of the slamming front door and Gina stomping down the stairs, it didn't seem like our Ms Grey needed any help at all. She popped her head around the door before Lucy had even got to it to go and help.

'You are all of you girls, right?' Ms Grey asked with a big grin, not looking as ruffled as I thought she would be. We all looked back at her, stunned, and nodded and giggled. Even Samantha laughed.

Orgy

It hadn't been a great week but, then again, it hadn't been a bad one either. The money had been good – I'd been busy, worked every day and, on most days, had two bookings, but they had all, without exception, been with a Mr Average. All of the clients had been quite old, too, and giving hand relief and compensation sucking to keep them up was beginning to get on my nerves. There hadn't been one good hard shag from one of them, and it was driving me nuts. And it doesn't help when it's that time of month when your hormones are making you crazy.

It was the weekend, and a call to my black bodybuilder was more than overdue. At least he might be able to tide me over until the following week, when, hopefully, I might at least get some good, hard, paid-for sex.

'House party? Why do you want to go to a house party? I was talking about coming around to mine and getting jiggy with it.' There was I, lounging on my sofa, nursing a cuppa in one hand and my phone in the other, wishfully thinking of diverting him from the gym and into my bed for an afternoon of romping about, and he wanted to go off to some silly house party that evening. What kind of man was he! I was not amused.

'It's a kind of open-house party for couples – you know, the ones that want to play . . . a swingers' thing.' He mumbled the last bit, and it all started to click. I must have sat up suddenly as I yelped, spilling tea all down me.

'You OK?' He sounded concerned. 'It's all right, there's no need to yelp. My mate has been before, and the guy who's running it is solid. If you don't want to stay, we can leave.' He was trying his best to sound convincing.

'So it's an orgy then?' I said it deadpan, images racing around my head. My afternoon was picking up, after all, and even though I sat there dripping with tea, I now had a huge grin on my face.

'Well, sort of, yes. I thought we could go and watch. I'm going with my mate – he knows I'm married so I can't join in. Can't have him have that info to use as ammunition against me, now can I?' He droned on about watching, and what his mate had said, and how he hadn't been to one before and wanted to go and see ... Bla bla bla.

All I could think about was how horny I was feeling and how watching was not going to cut it. 'So,' I butted in, 'what does your friend look like?' I had a niggling feeling this friend of his wasn't so much a friend as an acquaintance, as what kind of mate would blab to his mate's missus?

When evening came I dressed in my silk wrap dress, which I had mended after its fag-burn 'accident', and put on my nice see-through net Agent Provocateur lingerie, which some enthusiastic client had bought me. I was all set. I was trying to figure out how many condoms I could fit in my clutch bag in addition to my make-up, but I gave up and tipped the lot out on to my bed, grabbing my bigger, work handbag, which would hold everything I might need. How many condoms does a girl need at an orgy? Just in case, I put ten in the side pocket. I had no idea if they would supply any at this so-called house party. I added another ten just to be sure. What if they didn't have any there – would others need some too? I settled on thirty of different sizes. That should do it. I was horny, but how much free sex can one girl get at an orgy?

Quite a lot, was the answer to that one, as I found out …

The ominous, dodgy-sounding house party was being held in a normal-looking three-bedroom house in a run-down area in east London. It was hosted by a Jamaican gent in his late forties, his body still firm. He worked out in the same gym as Tony did and was very pleasant to talk to. We stood in the kitchen and chatted.

It was still early evening, and quiet. The house was scattered with white suburban middle-aged-housewife types and husbands who looked like bank managers. A couple was making out on a sofa in a dark corner, from what I could see. Our host was about to give us a guided tour of the top floor when we were joined by Desmond, Tony's mate, the one who had invited him to the party in the first place. He was a tall, wiry black guy in his late twenties, nothing special to look at, but from the bulge in his trousers he looked like he had an anaconda down his pants. I was intrigued. He was very friendly and more than interested, towering above me and flirting like mad, making one risqué pun after another, which made me laugh. If Tony was on his best behaviour, then this Desmond might have to do.

Tony had already hinted he would like to watch us. I excused myself to find the loo, and when I came back he grinned at me and suggested that Desmond show me around, as he was still chatting to our host about a body-building competition that was coming up. I was more than happy to do as he suggested and, in more ways than one, explore with Desmond.

I slyly hitched my dress a little higher as I was ushered up the stairs in front of my guide. He now had a good view up my skirt and, from the way he went quiet, I could tell it had drawn his attention. We heard a gurgled scream at the top of the landing and made our way to a doorway at the far end. We sneaked a peek around the frame, and we could make out an older couple going at it on the sheeted bed. The room, like the others, was lit with candles on the side tables and windowsills. There was enough light in the gloom to discern another couple sitting in chairs at the end of the bed, transfixed, watching the older gent slowly fuck, I presumed, his wife, as she gestured to a dreadlocked chap in the corner, who was merrily wanking away, to join them on the bed. He was over there like a shot and, no sooner had he loomed over the bed than the woman being screwed on it hung her head over the side and sucked his cock into her greedy mouth.

'Love a good spit roasting,' or something to that effect, was mumbled in my ear, as I felt the tall, dark, bulging body of Desmond behind me. He slid his hand up my dress and rubbed it over my hip and down my suspenders as we watched as she was rammed into by both men, both ends.

Not long afterwards, we checked out the other rooms. The second bedroom contained another bed and an older man and a chubby woman. They were against the wall, her on her knees giving him head, but the room wasn't well lit enough to be able to perve on the couple. The third room was empty, with a big king-sized bed in the centre with a fresh sheet, and surrounded by more candles. There were a few chairs up against one of the walls. It didn't take long to unwrap my dress and lay it over the table, and to get my rubbers out ready. Just in case, I fished out a bigger-sized one from the pile and slid it into my stocking top. I turned to find Desmond had taken off his shirt and was now hopping out of his jeans, clad in his socks and his boxers. He crawled across to me on the bed. It didn't take him long to peel my net knickers off and clamp his mouth to my crotch and lick away. His tongue darted in and out. Soon, my moaning had drawn the attention of other couples, who came to see what was going on.

Desmond was now on his knees on the floor at the side of the bed and I was sprawled over it. I was pinned down at the waist, exposed to the glances of the couples leaning at the doorway. I wasn't alone for long on the bed. It gave as our host sat down on the corner. He raised his eyebrows questioningly, his hand hovering over my nearest breast, and I nodded. I was happy for him to join in. I hadn't had two men before. Two girls, yes; two black girls, yes, that, too, in the past; but certainly not two black men.

I couldn't see Tony anywhere but I wasn't too bothered. Our host lowered his head and, after pushing aside my net bra for better access, sucked my nipple, only to be joined by another black head, who started doing the same on my other nipple. The third man, I guessed from the looks they gave each other, was a friend of the host. Three men? Why not? I was feeling slightly giddy as it was from Desmond's administrations. He, after some lengthy cunt-munching, had relinquished my now sopping pussy to our host, and I rubbered up the now boxer-less Desmond and sucked him hard, trying not to choke on his long cock. At the same time I rubbed the now very prominent bulge at the zip of the third man. Hands were everywhere, stroking me, probing me, plucking me gently.

I was in no mood for being licked out any longer. I wanted the long cock that was trying to choke me to fill another hole, the one that was sopping wet from the licking out I had just endured. They might have out-numbered me, but I was very much in control, which is what I wanted. I wanted them to be at my fingertips. I was flipped over on the shadowily lit bed by all the black hands that were on my skin and was filled instantly with a long hard stroke that made me shudder. I reached for another rubber, ready to suck our host's cock, which had just swum into view. Another cock sprang forth from the third man, next to my hand as he sat on the bed close to me. I was on all fours. I leaned heavily on one arm and used my other hand to pull off the meaty cock below me as I was rammed into from behind and sucked the second man's cock.

It was a jumble of legs and arms, and we were soon joined by a dreadlocked head and a prominent cock on the other side of the bed. I took a liking to it; we had been joined by the young chap who had been in the other room. Four I counted, and that was enough. With me as a satellite in the centre, I took it in turns to fuck, suck and wank each cock until I was done with all of them. As I made the last guy make me come, riding him hard to finish him off, too, I spotted Tony, a huge grin on his face.

Three hours it took, from what I could tell, to finish them all off, and I was thoroughly, literally, knackered. I was surprised I wasn't feeling more uncomfortable. I was content, but I was definitely shagged out. I drifted out of the door on Tony's arm, Desmond following behind and thanking our host briefly as we left. The other men had disappeared into the crowd, both saying thanks beforehand, also with big grins on their faces, which made me feel very pleased with myself.

After dropping Desmond off at a tube station, I drove Tony back to his and sat in the car park wanking him off as a goodbye and thanks for the evening. He looked even smugger than I felt at the fact that I had just tag-teamed the only four black men at the party, and he had been able to watch. That was one unexpected experience that I could tick off my mental list.

13. *Scarlet*

'That is *it*.' I threw my shag bag down on the sofa. I had picked Layla up from her agency, and on the drive back she had been nattering about the goings-on at her work. While I listened I pondered over what had happened at mine. I had kept it in for the whole journey, but now we were back at my flat, I couldn't any longer.

'I have *had* enough, that guy was just creepy. That's three in a row, and it's not even the end of the week yet. If I get any more "Oh haven't you got young girl's tits" I am going to vomit on their cocks.' I looked at Layla as she plonked herself down on the other end of the sofa to kick off her heels.

She patted my knee reassuringly. 'Oh dear,' she said, and gave me a look that didn't reassure me at all. She looked concerned. I was waiting for the 'You still get weirdos even if you do have bigger tits' speech, but it didn't come. She looked me in the eye with a firm frown. 'You're serious, aren't you?'

I was serious about the weirdos who like small, hardly there, child tits: they exist. I sat myself down on the sofa next to her with a thud. It was late and I had spent a good hour being bounced on some old codger's knee and then having my 'little-girly titties', as he called them, spunked over. It wasn't that I minded having them covered in spunk, but the way he went about it grated on my nerves.

Layla turned sideways to face me as I grabbed the TV remote to see if anything was on that might distract me from the thoughts pressing on my mind, hoping to forget the vile client I had just seen. But Layla was not making it easy.

'No, I'm not talking about the weirdos. You're thinking of a boob job, I can just see the cogs in your brain turning,' she muttered.

I muttered back. 'What have you got against boob jobs? All that research I've done has just gone to prove that it's not as bad as either you or I thought.' Layla had grudgingly come with me only the week before to check out a clinic that did the procedure. I'd had a feeling she'd been humouring me, thinking that if I went and heard all the gory details I would change my mind and decide against it.

I had decided against that clinic, but not about having the operation. It had taken five solid months of saving, and I now had a big pile of carefully folded notes sitting ready in envelopes in my locked moneybox if I needed it. It hadn't taken as long as I thought it would to earn the money, and now my mind was set. Having done the research, all I had to do now was to find a good surgeon and a hospital that let you stay overnight and didn't send you home straight afterwards, as some of them did. I didn't like the thought that, if anything went wrong and I was sent straight home, I would be stranded miles away from medical help. North London wasn't the middle of nowhere, but it was at least forty-five minutes to an hour to most of the hospitals and clinics which did the 'augmentation', and that worried me. What if the stitches came undone? Or it popped? Or I passed out, haemorrhaged, and even after Layla had called an ambulance it couldn't get me to a hospital on time? And as I had a rare blood group, what if they didn't have the right blood for a transfusion?

I might be set on having the operation, but I didn't take it lightly. It wasn't as if I had just woken up and thought, Oh I have the money: I want to get noticed and having bigger boobs is a good idea. I knew I didn't want big, fake-looking pornstar boobs and, from all the research, I knew they weren't all like that. I just wanted to look in proportion, look normal. Not all fake boobs were hard balloons, that was only the bad ops; the ones that got capsular contracture, the tightening of the scar tissue around the implant, were the ones that looked worst. If you had a good surgeon, then after a few months of them settling, no one should be able to tell and, if I was lucky and didn't go too big, no one would be able to feel either. Fingers crossed.

So began three weeks of searching, making a list and going to speak to the doctors on it. Some of them kept on and on about the scar being underneath the breast and, as I was determined to have the scar in my armpit so no one would be able to see it, I crossed them off straight away. At last I found one doctor, at a private hospital – I had to pay for a consultation even to speak to him – who had moved on from inserting implants from underneath the breast. Although he could put them in under the arm, for hygiene reasons, he claimed the best way and the way he had been doing it for some time was through the nipple. Then the crescent scar on the edge of the aureola would blend in and nobody would be able to see it. He was also using cohesive silicone, saying it was more stable than the saline. It did feel very soft and strong. Before I left his office he said I really didn't need it done, and I decided then that he was the doctor for me. Layla, after sitting in with me, still wasn't too sure but was resigned to the fact that I was determined now to go ahead and said she would take a week off to look after me.

The big day arrived. I had left the agency, telling Ms Grey that I needed some time off and that I would call her if I needed to come back. Only a few girls knew I was going to have the op, and only Layla knew that, afterwards, if I did go back to work as an escort, I wasn't going to work for Ms Grey. With my new, bigger boobs I would go to work at Layla's agency, as it paid better.

I was all set. I had got everything ready in the flat for when I came back, stocking up on food and other necessities, as I wasn't sure when I would be able to drive again. I did, though, fill the car with petrol and oil, just in case I needed it. I made my bedroom extra comfortable for my return and had packed drawstring trousers and front-fastening tops in my overnight bag, knowing I wouldn't be able to raise my arms above my head for at least a week after the op. Morbidly, I had even written goodbye letters to all my family and left them for Layla in a drawer, to post in case anything went wrong.

I arrived at the hospital in a cab with Layla at 7 a.m., way too early for my 10 a.m. prep time, and waited around nervously until I was shown to my room and settled in, ready to wait, and wait. I wasn't the only patient on the wing – at least eight other women were having the same op that day. 10 a.m. came and went and, after a few emergencies that the doctors had to deal with, I was still waiting. I had gone without food and, with more difficulty, water for over twelve hours by the time it was noon, and in the end I had to wait until 5 p.m., when they were finally ready to send me in. By that time I was too hungry and thirsty to be nervous and just wanted it over and done with. Layla was nervous enough for both of us and kept on disappearing for a smoke.

Next I knew I woke up in the recovery room with the two other ladies who had been wheeled in before me. I had seen them go, as they had been wheeled past my room. I was nearly sitting upright before a nurse realized I had come to from the anaesthetic and settled me back down again. I was a bit disorientated and didn't really even notice the bandage around my chest; I was more worried that I was awake and perhaps I shouldn't have been. But it was nothing to worry about, so the nurse said, I had just fought the anaesthetic off harder than the others. They wheeled me through the corridor and put me in my bed. I drifted off, waking some time later to find Layla watching a game show and eating the Hobnobs she had bought me. She smiled: everything was OK; it all had gone well.

I couldn't feel a thing. I was a bit stiff and my throat was dry because of the tube that had been put down there to help me breathe but, all in all, I felt fine. Wasn't that a bit strange? Everything I had read had said it was going to be painful and that I wouldn't be able to move for weeks.

The bandages around my chest didn't look as impressive as I had thought they would either, although I was wrapped up like a mummy from the top of my chest to around my ribs. Well, at least I didn't look like some sex-toy blow-up doll. That was a relief, especially as I had trusted my surgeon to gauge the right size on the day. Tired, Layla would only leave to go back to the flat and get some sleep when I proved I could actually stand and go to the loo with no effort and could even lift my arms a little. She left, her eyes weary, and waved, claiming she would be back at 9 a.m. the next morning, when I would be discharged, to take me back to the flat to recover.

It was nearly 10 p.m. by the time she left and that was almost my downfall, as I decided that, as I could get up, I would clean my teeth, as my mouth felt furry. Everything was fine – I was able to lift my arm a little and lower my head to clean my teeth, and then I climbed back into bed to get some sleep. I was very excited that I now had boobs, so I didn't drop off straight away. After a good half-hour I found that my right boob was hot to the touch. It didn't feel right: I knew there was going to be some swelling but should it feel like a mini coffee per-colator in my chest? No, I had a daunting feeling that I might be having some internal bleeding. I reached for the buzzer, only to be told by the very unhelpful nurse who turned up in response that swelling was to be expected and to ring again in a couple of minutes if it got worse. Of course it did get worse, a lot worse, and it was becoming very uncomfortable, having swollen in the tight bandage by the time the doctor was called back in. They had to operate again.

I had been given morphine for the pain, so I didn't feel much afterwards, and was just relieved to know that they had fixed the problem. I was pestered throughout the night, with nurses coming in and waking me up every hour to stick a thermometer in my mouth.

When morning came a new shift of nurses came on, and the one responsible for my room hadn't read my notes and didn't know I had been under again. She assumed that, because I wasn't speaking, I was just being difficult and deliberately wouldn't sit up for her. She stupidly didn't realize that I wasn't able to speak because of all the anaesthetic tubes that had been stuffed down my mouth and I couldn't sit up because I was still too weak. At that point, I couldn't raise my hand off the bed, let alone sit up. She gave me my drugs and I threw up all over her as she tried to get me out of bed. She went to get help, and it was only after a nice nurse came in and helped me eat and drink some water that I felt a bit better and was able to talk and tell her what had happened.

By the time Layla walked in I was dressed but still very pale, weak and ill-looking. She didn't know I had gone back into the operating theatre and under a second time and was intent on getting me back to the flat. By then, the wing was clear of people, as all the other ladies had left. None of them had had any problems. I checked myself out, not waiting for the nurse to come around and fit me with a support bra. The doctor wanted me to come back in three days for a check-up as it was. It wasn't as if I was too banged up; I only had a wraparound bandage for support.

I had already seen the small neat scars and my new boobs that morning, when the doctor had unwrapped the bandages. Despite the slight swelling from the right boob, which had been operated on again, they looked great. Even Layla was impressed when she saw them. My new boobs were two cup sizes bigger than they had been but still smaller than hers, but she had just imagined for some strange reason that they were going to look like cartoon boobs.

It was two days before I felt better, much quicker than I thought it would be. I had, against doctor's orders, been moving around and moving my arms too, slowly, as I reasoned I had already had a close call, so if it happened again I would know what to do and, also, I had read an article by some American that said if you didn't move a bit after the surgery, your muscles tightened up as you healed and you might not get back the movement you had before. The swelling had gone down and the scars were healing nicely. Apart from the small plasters on my nipples, they looked normal. I really hadn't expected to heal so fast and have no pain, especially as I had haemorrhaged and had to go under again.

By the second day I could not only push myself up out of bed without any problem, but I had no pain and could raise my arms above my head to put a T-shirt on. My new boobs were wonderful, better than I had expected. All the dresses I hadn't been able to wear before because they looked silly on me now looked great. I filled out the tops as well as the bottoms of things now – all curvy and in proportion. By the third day I could even drive to the hospital with no problem at all. Layla came with me but immediately went off in search of coffee. I sat and waited with another lady, who looked very uncomfortable, so I asked if she wanted a hand taking off her coat. She had had the same op on the same day as me but wasn't healing as fast; she was amazed I could lift my arms. Then she said that we were the lucky ones, as she had heard that some poor girl had had to be rushed back in that night. She was even more amazed to find out that it had been me. A few more ladies came in to wait for their check-up too. They were stiff and looked like they were in pain, and I really began to appreciate how lucky I was to have healed so well.

After being told off by the nurse for moving around as I was, and for having taken off my bandages, and getting an earful for not wearing my support bra, I left, having been fitted by the matronly butch nurse with the most lumpy, uncomfortable sports bra imaginable. It stayed on for all of an hour, until Layla and I had raided every lingerie shop I could find from there back to my flat. With new lingerie and new boobs, I felt like a new woman. And it wouldn't be long before I could start with a new agency, and with a new name: Scarlet.

'You'll like it here,' said Layla. She was showing me around her agency and introducing me to a few of the girls. It wasn't so bad being the new girl here, as at least I already knew someone and, because Layla was such a sweetie, she was well liked, which made it easier for me to fit in.

My first few weeks there were very busy; I hardly

had time to sit down and chat to any of the girls as I was dashing in only to be sent out again.

On average, I was seeing nicer clients here than in the last agency I had worked at, but I wasn't sure if it was because of the agency or because my new boobs were scaring off the nasty paedo clients I usually got.

I was getting a whole different type of gent, one who wanted the busty, bouncy blonde look rather than the little girl next door. I really noticed the change. It was far more fun at this new agency, too; the men were happy-go-lucky rather than demanding and our boss, Ms Lush, didn't send me to clients who wanted things I didn't do.

She was far more on top of her game than Ms Grey had been and noticed and heard everything that went on. It really didn't take long to settle in at all, which was good, as Layla was soon going back to uni again. She had been putting it off, feigning illness, but now it was time to go and tie up a few loose ends there, ready to pack up at the end of her term and come back to stay in London permanently.

Ice Maiden

'I don't get it,' Anita was saying. The tall blonde swung her new Louis Vuitton bag down on to the coffee table and herself into the spare place on the sofa.

Tandy looked up from her newspaper and over in acknowledgement at the glacial Swede who was now sitting next to me. Anita threw her hands up in the air and hrumphed, obviously wanting everybody's full attention.

''E complained, da bastard,' she huffed again. ''Ow dare 'e!'

Tandy put her paper down. 'OK. We give up. Who?' she asked, trying to contain a grin. Sonya was leaning on the doorframe. We were all now staring at Anita, who was flicking her hair back, away from her new Armani suit.

'Dah last punter, 'e phoned the Lush and complained, and I, I do nothing wrong!' She waved her hand.

It was early evening and, as per normal, Anita, and her perfect long legs, blue eyes and beautiful face, had been picked by the first guy who had walked in, as soon as he had heard she was Swedish – without even talking to her first.

Anita was always a popular pick. She could have gone on the catwalk, with her classic Nordic looks. She had come back from her booking scarcely an hour from when she had been whisked off, and there had still been an hour to go.

'What did he complain about?' Tandy asked warily. Anita shrugged, like she didn't really know.

'So what happened?' I just had to ask. Anita didn't normally talk about anything other than shopping, or how much something she had just bought had cost, other than to whinge that her rent was due and she was short of cash.

At that point the Lush called down the stairs and told me one of my regular favourite Mr Averages had phoned and would be in to collect me. She smiled at me from over the top of the stair rail; she didn't even look at Anita.

Anita straightened her back and fought for attention

as Ms Lush stomped off back up the stairs to her desk in her office.

''Appened, what 'appened?' Anita bristled beside me, looking down her nose. 'Well, nothing that doesn't normally 'appen. We go to 'e'ss, 'e offer me drink, I say no, and find bedroom, I take off my tings, give him rubber to put on and lie on bed so he can do dah business, he do sex, I get up go shower, ask him for taxi fare and come back here.'

She shrugged, and I raised my eyebrows at Layla, who was leaning on the kitchen door stirring her tea on the other side of the room. She had come in to listen.

'I do not understand, I thought this one OK, I thought this one at least might call and see me again.' She turned to me. ''Ow come you get punters that come see you again? What you do?'

Layla pushed off the wall and plonked herself on the arm of the sofa next to me and handed me a cuppa. She looked over my head to Anita and answered, not quite as diplomatically as I would have done. 'She wouldn't give the guy a rubber and make him put it on, for a start, let alone just lie there.'

I nearly spat my tea out, hearing her lord it over Anita.

Anita didn't look at all perturbed. ''Ow else would you get them to wear a rubber, but give them one? Some don't 'ave and I not touch their dirty dick.' She looked disgustedly at Layla. I heard Tandy titter.

Anita looked back down at me. 'You must do some other service to make them come back – what you do? You kiss, do it twice?' Anita looked really baffled, and Layla chuckled.

'Er, no, pretty much the same as you, but we chat a bit first, have a drink, then I give them a massage to make them relax,' I answered.

I was just starting to understand why Anita, as beautiful and perfect as she looked, didn't get call backs like the rest of us did. She survived by being picked first and more often, because of her looks and her nationality, but it sounded as if her cool personality and attitude was something that no one desired twice.

Anita looked at her perfect manicure. 'Who has time to do dat? Chitchat? Massage? They only just paying for a fuck!' She hrumphed again, shaking her head and tossing her long hair.

Tandy winked at me and rasped, 'Yes, they pay for our *time*, but there are ways to fuck and ways to give pleasure.'

Anita didn't sound like she got it. 'But that what I do – they have pleasure from fucking me. I lie there, they fuck me. Sometimes I even get on top, if they not ugly and fat.' I could feel more than hear Layla giggling behind me, as I tried to keep a straight face. 'Humph ... I being serious!' Anita grabbed her gleaming shoulder bag off the table. 'I need box of fags.'

In a puff of Chanel No. 5 she got up and stomped off up the stairs to go to the shop, not even asking if anyone wanted anything – not that she ever did think to ask anyhow.

'Poor Anita,' Tandy tittered as she got back to her paper.

'Poor Anita my arse.' Layla was in tears of laughter.

As soon as the front door closed, we all erupted into giggles.

Tuesday 3 p.m.–2 a.m.

Clients × 1 = Mr Slimeball

1 × 2 hours = £270

+ cab-fare tip = £20

Total = £290

– agency fee £70

– cab fare £4 (cab back)

Total = £216

'Here you are, Susan!' He looked thrilled at finding me at a different agency. 'You know Scarlet?' he queried, and I nodded. He didn't look confused at all, just beamed back at me. Mr Slimeball, my Italian cunt-muncher, had tracked me down from my other agency to this one. And I wasn't too happy about it.

'Puff! You just left. I ring around all the agencies to find you, it take ages. The other girls, they are not you, bella. I missed you!' And on he went, pleased as Punch that he had found his 'favourite redhead', so he said, despite the fact that my hair was now much lighter and strawberry blonde. He didn't even notice that my boobs were bigger – mind you, I doubt with the months that had passed he would have remembered, especially as that wasn't exactly where his interests lay. Had I thought having bigger boobs would have put him off, I would have told him, but I couldn't be bothered. I should have known better than to think that I could lose him just by changing agency. I had told some of my favourite clients at the old agency that if

I left and went to another agency, it would be this one I was working for now. It was Sod's law that the ones I didn't want to see and hadn't told would be the ones who found me.

It wasn't long before I was flat on my back in his bed, at his flat. He had been so enthusiastic about finding me again that I hadn't even had time to take my shoes off, let alone my dress – he had just pushed it up and torn away my knickers, which were in his way, before snuffling between my legs.

'Bella, you know what I would like to do?' His question didn't need an answer; in between dribbling, he was already telling me. 'If I could, I would love to mount your juicy pussy in a frame, with the rest of my art, just your ass and legs apart sticking up, tie your ankles to the corners of the frame, mmmm.' He grunted and rubbed his whole face in my sopping lips, now filled with his drool, and carried on with his mumblings. 'You open, come dripping out, hung in my hall! So I can lick you every time I pass.' He was over-excited now, and more than content at the task he had set himself, which was to make me come at least eight times before I left. I was not best pleased at having to fake it that many times, all the screaming and heavy breathing I was going to have to do, and all to his slobbering and running commentary about what he had wanted to do to me while I had been out of his grasp. I let out a fake gasp to keep him content until he was ready to come.

As ever, there are always the clients that none of the other girls want to see, usually because they are rough, nasty or condescending – not enough to be a risk, enough that no one would choose to see them.

Once, a girl I was working with recognized a voice and then a face through the gap in the door upstairs in reception as belonging to some chap she didn't want to see again and faked stomach cramps, saying that her period had just come on, in order not to have to say hello to him. She told us how rough he had been with her during a booking only four days before and showed us the finger bruises on her thigh to prove it. She'd said she wasn't going to see him again, as rough sex wasn't what she was into – even if her rent *was* due.

And she wasn't the kind of girl to pass up on the pound signs, so after that, we all gave him a frosty reception. He left in a huff, after we each of us mumbled our name and said our hellos half-heartedly and rudely, not making eye contact and looking around the room as if he wasn't really there, hoping he wouldn't pick us.

He left without choosing anyone, to try elsewhere, complaining about the rude reception he'd been given. When Ms Lush heard, she stormed down the stairs with a frown to ask what our little display had been about and looked straight at the girl, who hadn't said even a rude hello.

The girl looked straight back at her, and Ms Lush's eyebrows rose, quick off the bat, comprehension dawning in her face. She asked, 'Is that him?' And when the girl nodded, Ms Lush shrugged her shoulders and said, 'Oh,' before padding back up the stairs to answer the ringing phone.

'Has anyone got any mouthwash?'

Layla and I were sitting on the sofa at the agency watching some late-night movie. We probably weren't going to see the end of it, considering that the phone up in the office was ringing every five minutes. It was going to be a busy night. We hadn't seen the new girl much. Being both new and young, probably all of the eighteen that was on her card, not marked a few years down like most of us (I was currently still nineteen despite another birthday having just passed), she had been very popular. Even that afternoon she had already been whisked off as soon as she had arrived by a regular who wanted to 'try her out'. You can guess that I was beginning to find that phrase a little demeaning by now, can't you? Luckily, I had done my baptism-of-new-girl fire by then. But here she was, asking whether anyone had any mouthwash.

'You didn't let him kiss you?' Sonya had demanded of her as she plopped herself down on one of the chairs. But no, that wasn't it. From what we could gather, she couldn't get used to the condom and its taste. She had tried to suck him without, but the guy had complained he didn't want to catch anything, so she had to use the rubber. When she said that she had tried to suck him without one, the whole room went deathly quiet. Not using a rubber when you gave a blow job was a risk – a smaller risk, but still a risk. A working girl or escort with any sense knew that, and that risks just weren't worth taking – after all, it's not as if this job comes with sick pay. If you get ill, you don't earn and, on top of that, everyone considers it your own stupid fault, whether it is or not.

Any working girl who regularly attends a sex clinic, reads all the info and then gets lectured to death by the nurses is more than clued up. They almost scare you off having even protected sex, let alone considering doing oral without. If you didn't protect yourself, you just had no respect for yourself, was the general view. In a roomful of feisty women, in the clinic or in the agency, you just wouldn't argue the point.

The new girl had made a huge faux pas and she didn't even know it. Even if a girl did give oral without a rubber she would never admit to it. She knew all the other girls would think she was an idiot.

Layla asked what kind of condom she was using and the new girl tipped out the ones she had left in her bag on to the table. Layla sifted through them and gave her a quizzical look: the daft girl had been giving head with a normal spermicidal condom – no wonder she didn't like the taste. Nonoxynol-9 ones are like sucking toilet cleaner. And I thought the spermicidal ones would make your mouth go numb if you used them a lot – not that I ever have: I'm not that kind of girl, after all. I didn't use them and I knew Layla didn't either. From experience, both of us knew that using them more than twice for sex in one day could make your pussy sore and sting. Even for sex, we used the non-spermicidal ones. Anyone who used the spermicidal ones for oral couldn't be very experienced, didn't know her rubbers and probably hadn't even been to a sex clinic. And the blow job she would give using one couldn't be worth a damn. Anyone can give head without using a condom – it doesn't take much skill to dribble on a dick – but they do say it takes a pro to give good head when the man is wearing a condom. And I suppose we do all probably get a lot more practice.

Virtually all of us at the agency went to the working girls' project in Paddington, apart from Anita, who paid a fortune every three months to be tested at a private clinic on Baker Street. She didn't want to mix with street junkies, so she said, although she had never been to the project in Paddington and had no idea what it was like. There was a free NHS-run project attached to the civilian sex clinic, and it might have catered for street girls, but they didn't really see the distinction there – at the clinic a whore was a whore was a whore. Full tests there were even more complete than at a normal GUM (genito-urinary medicine) clinic, appointments were easier to get, they didn't ask your name (you had a number instead), you were given a variety of free condoms (including flavoured ones) and they would even make you a cup of tea in the hidden working-girls-only lounge. Why wouldn't an escort go there? They even gave you free lube in handy little disposable packets!

We had known this girl was new but we hadn't until then realized she was a grass-green uneducated civilian. Poor girl – she hadn't even thought of flavoured rubber. The other girls who had been hanging about got back to what they were doing, but they were still earwigging as

Layla, knowing my passion for rubber, and knowing I had a stock lurking in my bag, got me to dig out some flavoured condoms the new girl could try. I handed over three chocolate-flavoured ones, which I didn't like, and a few tutti-frutti ones I wasn't too keen on either. Layla sat and took her through how to suck a rubber on, demonstrating with a dildo she had in her bag – she had guessed, rightly, that the girl was still doing the civilian roll-on-rubber thing – much to the amusement of some of the other girls who were all covertly watching, and one of whom I guessed was pretty much taking notes, going by the look of intense concentration on her face.

Toy Boy

Typical! Just as I had started to rely on Tony, my personal sex toy, to come over when I called him after a bad week or, rather, like this time, a bad month of sex, he was going to up and leave me in the lurch. I had got used to him being at my beck and call, relying on him coming over and my being able to tie his big frame to my bed and do whatever I liked to him – and now . . .!

'Bodyguard?' I had just rung to see if he would come over so I could have an afternoon of sitting on his face, only to find out he had taken a very well-paid job as a personal bodyguard to someone I had never heard of. He was going to be away a few weeks, he said, maybe more. I wasn't going to hold my breath. 'OK, bye then. See you when you get back.' I must have sounded distracted – I was already thinking about a trip to a Soho sex shop for back-up toys if he was going to deprive me of his body.

'Aren't you going to miss me?' he queried, sounding more hurt than I thought he would – after all, it wasn't like I was the one going away.

'Probably not. Might miss your cock though.' What the hell did he want me to say?

It wasn't as if he was mine or was ever going to be. He was way too spoilt on the woman front. He had told me that his wife did everything for him. As far as I could tell, she was submissive, and that was the wrong way for her to go if she wanted his respect. She slaved to look after him and he said she was a walk-over. She even scrubbed his back and fed him in the bath, for goodness' sake. If he was expecting me to pine for him like his wife so obviously would, more fool him. I was going to need a replacement – and sex toys, now that I myself had been well and truly spoilt, might just fill the gap.

14. *Mr Tux*

Wednesday 3 p.m.–2 a.m.
Clients x 2 = Mr Tux, Elderly gent
1 x 2 hours = £540
Total = £540
– agency fee £140
Total = £400

I had been in since 3 p.m., as Ms Lush always liked to have at least one lady in at opening time, not that any men would really come in on the dot, but give it half an hour and on occasion you might be lucky, like I had been today, with an elderly gent who was in a rush and had to get home to be on time for an early dinner. He had booked, with Ms Lush's help, a tatty room around the corner in the cheap hotel we all hated because it was dirty and damp. I was in and out in an hour, so I was back in the girls' lounge in no time at all. It was quiet, no other girls around to chat to, so I sat down with a cup of tea and a good book.

We all had to take it in turns as the early girl, as it was considered a bad shift, normally an extra few hours just sitting around pretty much by yourself, twiddling your thumbs. If you were in Ms Lush's bad books – say, if you missed a shift or were late paying in a fee – she would add an early call to your rota every day you wanted to work, or put you on the quiet shifts at the beginning of the week. There would be no chance of being given the ones you wanted. You had to work at least five days a week for her agency as it was. All the agencies had a compulsory minimum four- or five-day week, basically to stop you working for other, rival agencies at the same time and maybe taking clients with you. They wouldn't employ you if you wanted to work fewer days. The compulsory minimum at my previous agency had only been four days, but I had worked five or six.

I didn't mind doing the early shifts; I don't know why other girls didn't like them. Maybe, as well as it being quiet, they didn't want to be the first one in and have to clean up the girls' lounge from the night before. I would ask for early shifts especially, to the point where I came in at 3 p.m. most days. Ms Lush understood: by taking them I would get at least two or three more clients a week, and that added up. The other girls couldn't understand it, but I figured that I was just going to be sitting around at home reading or watching TV, so why not do it at work and maybe make some money? After all, if you got an early booking the client was unlikely to be drunk, was usually less trouble and, sometimes, you could even be back before the other girls arrived to start their own shift so they wouldn't realize you had just had a booking, and would be less likely to be jealous.

I had already been burnt by other girls' jealousy, and I didn't want it to happen again.

That day, I looked up from my book as two girls I knew well teetered down the stairs. I was a bit surprised as I knew they were not on the rota for that day. I nodded as they walked by to hang up their coats and shouted after them that the kettle had just boiled. That's strange, I thought, as a few more girls swept in, and the room started to fill up. Anita came last of all, dead on 6 p.m. By then there were eight of us, when normally only five were on shift at any one time. We all knew something had to be up. A few of the girls said they had been asked to come in because there was a party of gents booked in. How many, no one knew, but it must be a big group of important gents to get the Russian girls now in the corner to come rushing in on their day off. The Lush hadn't said anything when I came in, so it was news to me, but then again, she had been on the phone and had been talking away ever since – phoning all the girls and asking them if they wanted to come in, it seemed.

The doorbell rang just before eight and we could all hear that a big jolly crowd of men had come in. One was particularly loud and sounded like he had already started off the night with a bottle.

It was all quite exciting, but a bit scary too – we had never had such a big group of gents in before. Typically, they came in in twos; maybe five max for a stag party or a birthday; never as many as we could hear now, stomping around and then sitting down on the three Chesterfield sofas that lined the reception room.

'Bring in the wanton women,' bellowed the loud-mouthed gent from above. That was followed by some hearty chuckles – the men were obviously all in high spirits.

A few girls had snuck up the stairs to peek through the gap in the door to see what was going on. 'So, how many?' whispered Tandy when they were at the top of the stairs. We were deadly quiet getting ready – applying lipgloss, straightening stockings and slipping on heels.

'I see nine. Very smartly dressed – bloomin' bowties and everything' came the reply. The girl who had spoken had come back down and was dashing off to the back room to change out of her short clingy dress. Whisking back in sixty seconds flat, she wore a plainer knee-length red affair, which made her stand out from the other girls, most of whom were in their normal black. I was in my new long dark-blue dress so I didn't bother changing. It was slit to the side, low cut and clung to every curve. The other girls who had been at the top of the stairs were now rushing off to put a different dress on, also hoping to stand out.

Most of the girls would have at least two dresses with them. A short one was fine to say hello in, but sometimes gents liked us to wear something less conspicuous to leave and go to their hotel in, something longer and smarter looking. We all wore long coats which nearly skimmed the floor and hid a multitude of skimpiness underneath – that was only for the client, behind a hotel door for an hour or two – but that didn't matter: it made them feel less uneasy if you dressed a little more conservatively.

With that amount of men up there, it wasn't a matter of competing to get picked like in a normal line-up when you go to say hello one at a time, it was all a matter of catching the attention of the best gent and making sure he would pick you. The best gent was normally the one who had the most money and, on the whole, was the one in the group who did most of the talking. Usually, he had first pick, but that wasn't always the case. Sometimes he'd be paying for a friend, or someone he wanted to impress for some reason, and then he'd let the honoured guest pick first. The pack leader wouldn't always be easy to deal with but, looking at it from the money side of things, he was more likely to come back and pick you again, to tip you better or to recommend you to his mates.

'Right, who's going first?' piped up one of the girls.

OK, even I was a bit nervy as the men were still all rather loud up there, but none of the other girls looked as if they were going to volunteer. I raised an eyebrow, leaning on the newel post at the bottom of the stairs. The girls were by now sitting or standing to the sides of the room, but they were all looking up and straining to hear what was being said upstairs. 'Don't tell me you all have stage fright?' I huffed at them. Where was Layla when I needed her? Great time for her to go off back to uni and leave me to fend for myself.

'I'll go last, I need the loo,' said Miss Red Dress, and dashed off. Even Miss Brazil, who was usually the life and soul, was sitting in a corner painting a nail.

I tripped to the top of the stairs, and the girls fell in line behind me after much beckoning. Ms Lush opened the door and came face to face with me.

'Right, there are a lot of them,' she whispered to me. She looked over to her desk, where the phone had started to ring over the chatter. 'Get the girls to come in in fours and introduce them. Otherwise we'll be here all day, and they'll forget who's who by the time they've seen the last girl,' she said, and with that she was dashing off to her desk.

I took a deep breath. Hell, I had said hello to just as many men in the past, and in my undies – I'd even stripped naked on stage in a room full of them. Right, relax: it's only a roomful of rowdy men – how hard can it be to do it in a dress?

I swept the room with a glance – a bit like the way I clean my flat, really. I took note of the nine gents, all in various degrees of black tie, sitting three to each sofa, some perched on the arms.

'There you go – you love a busty strawberry blonde.' One of the gents nudged the gobby ruddy-faced man next to him, who was obviously the leader of the pack, the one we had all heard the moment he stepped in the door and plonked his big butt down centre stage in the middle of the room.

'Hello, love,' the pack leader said, patting his knee.

I put on my best smile and said, 'You haven't seen the other lovely ladies yet. Let me introduce them.' I turned to the door to introduce the next lady, but someone caught my attention. He was standing there, arms crossed, in a smart black fitted suit, a tenth man to the group.

I'm not normally taken aback by men – I see a lot of them all the time, of all shapes, sizes and ages – but this guy was stunning compared to his counterparts on the sofas. They all seemed very nice, but normal, the type that usually come in, an accountant, banker, a company director or two amongst them – they looked the sort, despite the black tie – and anything from early forties up to the refined-looking old chap on the end, who was easily in his seventies.

The tenth man was late thirties if that. He had jet-black hair, stunning blue eyes and a chiselled jaw, and looked as if he was over six foot tall. He had a smart gold watch on his tanned wrist. It's not every day you see a stunningly sexy gent in a black tux who looks like he's stepped out of a Monaco casino, especially not in our agency. It might have been a smart agency, but it wasn't that smart. I took another deep breath, hoping that my stare hadn't been registered.

Damn, he looked like he had seen a ghost. Oh dear, what had I done?

I looked away and back to the leching john, who was positively drooling now, staring at me and still stroking his knee. Bloody hell, I thought, why does this always happen to me? I bet Anita or one of the snobby Russians gets the guy by the door and I end up being slobbered over by this loud john.

I introduced the first four girls and they all gave their own hello, then went back down the stairs so there was space for the next lot of girls. Everyone made an effort, apart from Anita, who never did and couldn't see why she had to. When they left I followed them, leaving the group of men to the administrations of Ms Lush, who had just put down the phone in order to deal with the smart rabble's requests.

'Miles?' The loud john calling out could be heard through the door as we all gathered at the top of the stairs, once more straining to hear what was going on.

'Of course, dear chap. You still get first pick if you

want. She's on me, after all.' After that came much mumbling.

'They're going to take ages,' Miss Red Dress huffed as she stomped down the stairs. 'And after all that, I bet they only pick one of us.'

'Nah, nah, I looking hot tonight, I got new Louboutins! Ve all look hot. Ve all get picked,' pouted the tall Russian girl, digging around in her handbag to find and reapply her clear lipgloss. Anita grabbed her coat from the back room and draped it over the sofa ready.

We all sat down to wait while Miss Red Dress gave us an ever-developing running commentary on who was picking whom. From what I could gather, Miles, whoever he was, had picked me, and Anita had the loud john, much to her disgust and my mirth. Miss Red Dress was mentioned, and there seemed to be a choice going on between the Tall Russian or Miss Brazil – we could hear a booming male voice from above dithering between them.

The girls who had not yet been picked were then called to go up again so the other men could take another look. I got my coat and got ready to leave.

Four of us having been chosen by the first four men, the six men left only picked another two girls in the end, the older gents opting for a quiet night. We four were ready to go. As we passed the reception lounge I could see that the loud john and three others, including the handsome man in the tux, were no longer there. Apparently the four men who had picked us were champing at the bit, waiting for us outside, ready to catch taxis to the various hotels they were staying at. Their mates were still sitting around, two waiting for the girls they had chosen, and to pay.

The fees for a two-hour booking for the four of us had been paid for by the time we got to the front door, though I was still none the wiser as to which man I was going to go with. As I passed the desk, Ms Lush grabbed my arm to have a word.

'As you've already had a booking this afternoon, and your fees have already been paid, you don't need to come back. I have too many girls on now.' She smiled and gave me a meaningful look as I dashed out. I took it as an order rather than a request – she obviously wanted to keep the peace, and not to have too many pissed-off girls sitting around twiddling their thumbs the whole evening, especially as some of those she had called in specially on their day off had not been picked. She didn't need me coming back; she would have a full house to juggle on what was normally a quiet midweek night as it was.

There were two taxis standing on the kerb when I shut the agency door behind me. Two gents were already in one of them with one of the girls, and the loud john was hustling Anita into the other cab, along with Miss Red Dress and another dinner-jacketed man. I gathered rather than was told to get in the first cab and that I was to go back with the man called Miles. Waving to a disgruntled-looking Anita and Miss Red Dress, I climbed in the cab, sliding into the back seat just as a tanned hand reached over and shut the door before I could reach for it. Sitting in front of me on the pull-down seat was the brooding Mr Tux, although now his shocked look of earlier had been replaced with a soft smile. I smiled back a little and then broke into a full grin as I realized that Miss Brazil had her hand possessively high on the leg of the man next to her on the back seat.

Mr Tux was all mine. 'Hi, I'm Scarlet.' I took his hand and reached across the small gap, moving towards him to peck him on the cheek. 'Miles,' he murmured as I leaned back. My hand was still in his, and he placed it on his knee, stroking it casually with one of his long fingers. We didn't get to talk much, as Miss Brazil was quizzing them both about the function they had been to, which had been some boring business-award thing, which is why they were wearing dinner suits and bowties. It didn't take at all long to reach their hotel, it was only around the corner, and, anyway, I was far too distracted by the long, strong finger that was reeking havoc with the skin on the back of my hand and the sharp blue eyes that kept on flicking over me really to pay much attention. In any case, with Miss Brazil doing all the talking, there wasn't room to get a word in.

Before I knew it we had all got out of the taxi and she and I were being whisked across a shiny lobby floor on the arms of our clients and into the lifts. Miss Brazil winked at me as I followed the broad back of my client out of the lift when it stopped on the fifth floor. I winked back as, after my hunk of a client, she had the next-best-looking guy of the group. I followed my tall dark stranger down the corridor to his room. My palms itched in anticipation: I hadn't had a younger, cute man in quite some time and, after the disappointing sex from the earlier booking that day, I was now horny as hell.

I am the kind of girl who, the more sex I have the more I want, and this time it was working in my favour. If this guy wanted to sit around and talk before getting down to action, I didn't reckon his chances. As he opened the door to his hotel suite, I was already calculating how quickly I could get my dress off. I didn't even want to give him a chance to offer me a drink. He stood aside and ushered me in, and I walked straight over to the window, employing my usual tactic but this time pulling down the zip of my dress and letting it hit the floor before he was even halfway across the room after hanging up our coats. Going by the grin he gave me, he definitely liked what he saw, and he stopped in his tracks, starting to pull off his tie. I bent slowly to pick my dress up, looking up at him from under my lashes as he tugged away at the knot at his neck. I tossed my dress over the back of a chair and ambled over to the side of the big white bed to drop my bag on the bedside table. He followed, kicking off his shoes.

For a brief moment I could smell his musky after-shave, and then his tanned, strong fingers swept up my side and around my waist before I could take a breath and turn to face him. I noted the gold band glistening on his ring finger as I looked down to see his hand's progress, sliding up to cup my bra. The room was lit only by a desk lamp in the corner and, even though it was very quiet, I was being deafened by the pounding in my head, and by the sound of his ragged breath by my ear. Arching my back so my bottom made contact with his lap was all it took to confirm that there was a hard erection straining against his dress trousers. There was obviously no need to talk, our hands were set on exploring; there was no need to even pretend with formalities. In the taxi I had guessed he wasn't the talkative sort. The eyes that had been undressing me had told me all I really needed to know: he wanted me, and he knew I knew.

I turned to him as he unclipped my bra, and the hard, pink points of my nipples distracted him as I flipped the small buttons to undo his shirt, pulling it out from his waistband and running my hands up his muscled chest, which was speckled with rough hair, then over his shoulders, which flinched slightly, tightening, as I kneaded. Even if my mind hadn't been racing at that moment I couldn't have missed his lips as he brought them down and crushed mine in a kiss.

That brought me back down to earth. What the hell was I doing? He was a client – a damn sexy client, but a client all the same. I broke away gently, only to be caught by his firm fingers at my back bringing me down on his lap as he sat down smoothly on the side of the bed. My stockinged legs were either side of his firm thighs as I straddled him. Now that we were face to face, his eyes looked black, searing into me as I slid my hands down his chest, at the same time as he slithered his down my back and cupped my bottom, hooking his thumbs in my suspenders.

The side clips holding my stockings in place were dealt with deftly and, as I tried to focus, fiddling with his zip, he dipped his head and licked one of my now prominent nipples. My wriggling on his lap had made his cock bulge and strain even more to be freed from under the fabric. In the instant I pulled away to kick off my shoes and scoop up the condom that had fallen out of my stocking top, he had slipped out of his trousers and boxers. Propped back on his arms, his legs swinging off the bed, I had the condom on him and his cock in my mouth before he had time to take a steadying breath. He was larger than I thought, the bulge getting bigger as I sucked; even though he had been hard before, he was getting harder still. I eased back. I wasn't going to let him come yet – where would be the fun in that?

Firming my fingers round the base of his shaft with a slight pressure, I sucked more slowly as he thrust up, then swallowed a further few inches, drawing it out as long as I dared. My little black silk thong was still sliding down my leg as I crawled up over him, pushing him into the bed as he tried to move so his legs were on it. I hovered, poised over him, and sat up as his hands splayed over my hips, one finger dipping around and skewering my damp cunt before I had a chance to lean over his cock and have that take the finger's place.

He probed and teased, now with another finger, and I raised a knee and leaned over him, arms propped above his shoulders to hold my weight. He sucked my nipple as it came into his line of sight. The fingers explored and tickled, and his other hand turned my hip to rest on the bed as he struggled up. I forgot my job. I forgot about trying to slide down on his cock, I forgot to keep my eye on my watch, I forgot to keep his tongue out of my mouth. I was under him before I could blink, and his fingers were replaced with a pulsing cock. My eye jerked open, startled, as he filled me up to the hilt.

He was in less of a hurry than I thought and took

his time, slowly screwing me into the bed, every stroke pressing harder. Harder, and harder still, till his chest expanded with the effort of breathing and his body glistened under my palms. I came under him with a shudder, then he fucked progressively faster, soaking his cock as he made me even wetter. My pussy started to tighten from the friction. Frustratingly, he came in a surge before I could change our position so I could have him beneath me, where I wanted him.

It was only now, as he slumped over me catching his breath, that I looked at the watch on my wrist over his shoulder. I wanted more, I wanted him behind me doggie-style too. I peered at the dial. Damn, time was nearly up. He sat up and eased off on to his side, his hand draped over my hip, which was comforting. I tried to take my mind off the niggling thought of what his cock would feel like in other positions, what skill his tongue had and how it would feel between my other lips, as he leaned over to kiss and tease my bottom lip as we propped up on the pillows and began to chat.

Now he was more relaxed he was more talkative. I teased out the reason he had looked like he had seen a ghost when he first saw me. He said I resembled his first wife: I was the same height, had the same colouring: even the way I now wore my hair was the same. They had been sweethearts at school but she had died some years back in a bike accident. He had married again since but it wasn't working out. The business associates he had been with, who were out to impress him, trying to strengthen business ties, always brought him along when they went to pick girls at agencies, but he had never taken part. He had loved his first wife and been faithful to her, so he said, and in the second, rebound marriage, too – until I had walked in and reminded him of his dead lost love.

I didn't want to think about how much of what he was saying was a load of bull. It could have been worse. Reminding someone of a love lost had to be better than them thinking of you as a little girl. He was gorgeous, a good fuck and, to top it all, he was easy to get on with and understood my sense of humour. He looked at his watch, the only thing he was wearing, and commented on the time, saying it was a shame I had to go as I slid off the bed, grabbing my bag and heading to the bathroom to clean up. It didn't take long to shower and comb my hair back into place. It took longer wrestling with my libido: I didn't have to go back to the agency; there was no hurry; would he mind if I stayed longer? Noting the time, I took a deep breath and I fished my phone out of my bag. I dialled the agency as I left the bathroom, wrapped in a towel, to find my underclothes, in disarray all over the floor.

'Hi, it's Scarlet,' I said. I looked over to the bed, where the tanned, naked male body I had left there replete was lying still, arms crossed behind his head, feet crossed at the ankles. He surveyed me as I came out of the bath-room, phone glued to my ear. Ms Lush answered on the other end, a brief, irritated YES? I could hear girls bickering in the background.

'I have left the hotel and I'm on my way home. Yes, he was fine. See you tomorrow,' I went on, noting the time. My mobile went dead after a brief OK on the other end.

I turned it off and dropped it into my bag. Then I let my towel fall to the floor. That caught his eye. He stirred and stated the obvious, that I was still there, with a slowly raised eyebrow and a slowly rising erection. I only had to answer that I was now off the clock and that I couldn't go and leave him in that kind of state to have him easing up off the bed further and pulling me to him as I approached. His hands wrapped around me and eased my crotch to his face. I was soon more than content. I was right about his skilful tongue: it set to work and carried on till my legs couldn't hold me.

Morning came faster than we both expected and I hurriedly dressed and shrugged on my long coat as the phone on the bedside table rang.

I scribbled my number down on the notepad as he picked up the phone, answering and 'yes dear'ing to his wife on the other end. I blew a kiss across the room and pointed to the notepad I had left on the side. He frowned and quietly slid out of the bed, gently pulling the hotel-room door shut behind me so it didn't even click. My phone rang as soon as I was around the corner from the hotel, walking to the next street, where I had parked my car the day before. Fingers crossed, as it was still early, it wouldn't have been towed or got a ticket. We chatted as I walked, finding my car exactly as I had left it, safe and sound. I was so mellow after that, I agreed that we should meet again at some point in the future, much to the disgust of my professional, business-thinking brain – my libido was running amok through that.

Thinking about it logically, the sex had been great and,

what with Tony disappearing with no idea when he might be back, I might just have found a replacement. Mr Tux wasn't a brain, wasn't brawn, but if you can class a man as beautiful, he was it. Oh, and the chemistry helped, too, of course.

Remedy

Wednesday 3 p.m.–2 a.m.
Clients x 0
Total = £0

The girl who everyone affectionately called Gypsy had gone over to the new girl with her Tarot cards. The new girl didn't look happy; did she want her fortune told? She was looking a bit uncomfortable and was keeping herself to herself. She had been crouched in the corner of the lounge for a couple of hours and hadn't even got up to say hello to the last client who had come in. Eventually she told Gypsy that she was constipated, and Gypsy immediately started fishing crystals out of her handbag and coming up with all sorts of weird remedies.

Then everyone started chipping in their own piece of advice on the subject. It was a boring Wednesday evening – hardly any men call in midweek – and all the girls were settled in the lounge, whiling away the time until the next call. Only one man had come in in hours, and he'd changed his mind and 'walked'. The phone was so dead that Ms Lush had got one of us to phone the agency earlier, just to check it was working.

I looked up and over to the corner and added my

tuppence worth: 'Think there is some prune juice in the fridge if you need it.'

'Got some 'erbal tablets dat work,' said one of the Russians, diving into her Louis Vuitton bag.

'Are you drinking water? Try with olive oil in,' piped up the other Russian, watching TV and sitting next to her compatriot, who was now muttering what sounded like Russian swearwords and pulling all sorts of things out of her bag and on to her lap, trying to find her elusive tablets ...

'Senna pods, she needs senna pods,' said Tandy matter-of-factly, looking up from her copy of the *Financial Times*, which she was reading seated at the table. 'Oh, and some sit-ups – exercise works wonders.'

At a sit-in agency, the combination of sitting around for hours, followed suddenly by a lot of, shall I say, 'action', followed by lots more sitting down, the stress from clients and girls, the odd hours and having to grab any kind of food when you can get it (if you don't manage to bring some in) is not always good for a girl's constitution. It was common for the girls to talk about things like that, and slimming tips; everyone would chip in and try to help. This poor girl had only been working for two weeks, and as a truly new escort, not one touring from agency to agency to cash in on the new-girl trade. And as a newbie, she had not had much luck with the girls who had worked there longer talking to her.

She had survived her first busy two weeks and had been suffering in silence until Gypsy asked if she was all right. I was lucky – it hadn't happened to me yet. I had learned from one of the brothel girls I used to work with, and I never ate anything solid after 6 p.m., just soup, a pot of mashed potato if I was really peckish, or just tea or chewing gum. So far, that had worked a treat for me. Everyone thought it was strange, even Layla – but it did mean that my cans of soup and pots of ready-to-rehydrate potato sat safe in the cupboard, whereas a packet of chocolate Hobnobs never could be.

But thank heavens for the twenty-four-hour Tesco down the road in Knightsbridge! Otherwise I would have been grabbing fast food and eating take-aways like the other girls and ended up being in the same fast-food, slimming-pill, hire-a-trainer-down-the-gym, yo-yo-diet hell as every other girl I knew. Working nights and sleeping days, I tended to do my shopping at night after work. Layla always raided the fridge when she got back to my flat after work, and she was the biggest hoarder of laxatives I knew. She took them when she had problems, and I knew that constipation was a problem for most working girls in parlours. I just hadn't realized it was such a problem with nearly all escorts too, until it cropped up that day.

'Got them.' The Russian shook her herbal pills at the new girl.

I didn't know if the pained look on the newbie's face was because she hadn't been able to go to the loo in three days or how she was going to say 'thanks but no thanks' to the weird-looking, foreign-labelled pills; they could have had anything in them for all she knew. The newbie caught them when they were thrown across the room, not wanting to seem ungrateful, especially to the feisty Russian. 'Err, thanks,' she managed to say, slinking off to the kitchen with Gypsy in tow.

She left early that night after a chat to Ms Lush, saying she would come back when she felt better.

'That's the last we'll see of her. I didn't think she'd cut it,' slurred Ms Lush when we closed up later, and she was right. I didn't see her again after that evening.

Mr Arse-lover

Monday 6 p.m–.2 a.m.
Clients x 1 = Mr Arse-lover
1 x 2 hours = £270
+ cab-fare tip = £20
Total = £290
– agency fee £70
Total = £220

He bent me over the table and unzipped my skirt so it fell to the floor.

Picking up the lube, he squirted it in the crack of my bum and ran his spare hand down the inside of my leg and then up, rubbing the lube over my bum again and again until it was dripping all over his bedroom carpet. He had done a similar thing before, so I wasn't surprised he wanted to do it now. I bent over obligingly.

'There, you should see your arse – it's glistening now,' he said, standing back to admire his handiwork.

He dropped the lube to the floor and slid both hands up the insides of my legs, spreading them apart and sliding both his thumbs up into me. I took a quick breath as his fingers tickled my clit, making me quiver. He was making me come, and I was a bit dizzy as his fingers worked away.

'You have such a beautiful arse . . . did you know that?' He leaned over me, holding me over the desk, my legs splayed apart. 'Such a tight little pucker too,' he continued, sliding one of his fingers all too quickly up my bumhole before I had any idea what he was going to do. He hadn't done that before and it was a bit of a shock! I jumped, letting out a loud 'Ouch, what the fu–', making him topple backwards. I winced as he pulled his finger out.

'Sorry, I couldn't help it. You OK?' I looked over my shoulder and he looked back at me like a naughty schoolboy.

'Yes, I'm fine, just a bit of a shock. I can't do that, it's too small a hole.' I didn't add that it was too fucking painful.

'Yes, just like your pussy . . . tight.' He grinned, turning me on the desk edge and lifting my legs ready to enter me. I put my legs behind him and pulled him to me, sliding back and forth on the desk from all the lube. I was still a bit preoccupied about where his finger had been and I was trying to keep an eye on where it was now. I wanted to make sure he didn't touch my cunt and end up giving me a urinary infection because of it.

'We could do some arse training if you like? I can finger you till you're ready to take my dick, I can get some butt plugs, too, to stretch you. I will pay you an extra £1,000 to be in your virgin hole first. Please think about it.' He puffed as he came.

Ha, that will just have to be his fantasy, I thought! There was no way, even if I was desperate for the money, that his cock would fit. The money was tempting, and I had thought about it fairly seriously, but I wasn't sure I wouldn't pass out from the pain. It was the second time that month that some guy had wanted back door and mentioned the so-called pornstar experience, and that was unusual – it rarely happened or was even asked for. At this rate, it wouldn't surprise me if the clients wanted to kiss next, or that Ms Lush was for some reason sending me to A-level clients. I hoped she hadn't got my index card mixed up with someone else's, or that one of the girls hadn't marked my card out of spite. It wasn't unheard of for a girl's card to be changed when Ms Lush popped to the loo or had left a girl to look after the desk while she popped out to the off licence.

Mr Arse-lover waved me off after automatically giving me £20 for a cab back to the agency. I'd suggested that next time he see one of the crazy Russian girls, who might be more obliging. He nodded apologetically and grinned.

Back at the office, after being buzzed back in and my time noted, I asked to check my Rolodex card. It hadn't been changed. I was still marked as a normal escort and not highlighted in a fetish category.

15. *Lady of the Night*

I had seen him twice before already in the previous weeks. He really didn't want sex, and it was easy to work out that he was more of a voyeur. If he just wanted to watch and only really wanted a blow job at the end, it didn't bother me at all. The second time I had met him, he wanted a BJ in his car when he picked me up from the agency. He had a perfectly nice flat near by, but he confessed that it felt more illicit outside, albeit in a deserted, darkened street. I asked whether he cruised for girls in his posh car, but he said he never had, and made a point of saying that, weirdly enough, he had never harboured any thoughts about picking up a street girl; he didn't want to take that much of a risk. He was in his mid-thirties, just under six foot, fairly good-looking and smartly dressed; his suits were, if I judged correctly, custom-made. He was a nice gent. If he got his jollies in his very swish Lexus, which had tinted windows and an all-black interior, well, fair enough – at least it made a change from the monotonous hotel bookings for vanilla, average, run-of-the-mill sex with middle-aged men with glasses.

That second time, he had driven to the dark sidestreet and I had taken care of his needs after only about ten minutes; he was driving me back to the agency in no time flat. I was checking my hair in the passenger mirror when

235

he mentioned that he wanted to take me to a swinger's club. That caught my interest.

'Aren't swinger's parties for couples only?' I asked, now fixing my make-up in the mirror, thinking happily that, as it was early in my shift, I might get at least one other booking, or maybe two, out of the night, if I was lucky.

'Yes, but they won't know if we don't let on. We could pass as a couple. I'd just like to go and watch, that's all.' He parked up outside the agency.

'So, is it like a mass orgy then?' I queried back, thinking it had to be something like the house party I had gone to with Tony, which was the only thing I had to compare it to. The only things I knew about swinger's clubs really was second-hand info from the girls at work and from a few American movies. No one really talked about it, and even the clients who mentioned them were a bit vague.

'Umm, not really. If you come with me to check it out, you don't have to go off with anyone if you don't want to. I just want to watch and then do this again when we leave,' he said, pointing to his crotch. The guy was all class – as much as a guy that gets his rocks off in lay-bys can be, that is.

I nodded and we talked about meeting up the following week for a party he knew was taking place in a wine bar in the West End. I said he should call Ms Lush and organize it. He kissed me on my closed mouth and got out to open my door to let me out. He drove off as Ms Lush buzzed me in, looking at the clock on the wall and then smiling at me when I told her I had an evening booking the following week. I could see the pound signs in her eyes and wasn't surprised when I got the next phone booking, which came in an hour later. I swear Ms Lush could talk any man into anything on the phone – the gent who had phoned had been looking for an exotic, tall lady and ended up with me – and he gave me a big tip, too, when I left.

Mr Swing booked me for six hours the following Friday, a long booking for my agency, and well in advance, which was very rare. Most men called in at the last minute or, at most, the day before to book the lady they wanted. Ms Lush had informed me that my voyeur Mr Swing used to see one of the other girls, who had left the agency last year. The girl had had no problems with him and had gone with him to the clubs a few times but only for a few hours. She assured me he was a good client, but had only just come back; he'd been window-shopping at the agencies until he came across me.

It would have been nice to have known that before I first saw him, but I had worked out that it was easier to get info out of Ms Lush at the end of the night, when she was a bit pissed from the bottle she kept in her bottom drawer. Because I always drove home, it wasn't as if I had to dash off at the end of the night, and helping her lock up put me in her good books. Calculating? Well, yes, a bit, but if five minutes at the end of the day when all the other girls had dashed off got me the better bookings and meant she pushed me on the phone – hell, I wasn't there *just* for the sex, was I? Ms Lush wasn't stupid, she knew why I helped out. It wasn't quite ass-kissing – not like the girl who bought her a bottle of whisky every week as a gift – but it was noted.

'I like the way you help out, it shows respect. Most girls don't think, they're lazy. I know you'll be the same with clients, and that will bring their wallets back,' she said one night as she was locking the front door, then waved me off to my car.

Friday arrived and I went straight to Mr Swing's hotel, with Ms Lush's consent (Mr Swing had already paid by credit card). I arrived at his door feeling more confident than I thought I would and stood there in high heels and a fitted blue dress. He showed me into the small room, which had some boxes stacked on the bed. He had bought me a set of see-through net designer lingerie, which I was ecstatic about. I know it must have cost at least £200. It wasn't as if I didn't have some nice black satin undies on – I had quite a drawerful of sexy, slinky things by then; but nothing like that, nothing quite so expensive. The bigger box was a designer black silk wrap dress, which he said would make a good impression. I didn't like to mention I was a small not a medium and tied it as tight as I could. He didn't notice that it didn't fit too well. I modelled it for him and then gave him a blow job as a thank-you. I struggled to get his zip undone; we didn't have much time. He kept on saying that he wanted to get to the wine bar that was hosting the club night as soon as we could so as not to miss anything. Sex, he said, could always be taken care of later.

The boutique hotel he had booked was quite a few streets away from where the party was happening, so we climbed into his sleek black car, which was parked out front, drove the short distance and parked up on the street the bar was in. We went in, following a smartly dressed older couple. I felt a bit nervous. Was it going to be like a fetish club? Were there unknown rules here, too, that I should know about? Was it a general swinger's club, or were there, as I was beginning to suspect, different types of swinger's clubs? I knew that fetish clubs varied in the particular fetishes they catered for: there were parties for foot fetishists, gay fetish club nights, events that took place in cafés, without the clubbing atmosphere, rubber club nights – the list was as endless as the list of people's perverted persuasions. If you have a fetish, there's bound to be a club for it. Was swinging and swapping partners a fetish of sorts?

There was obviously quite a range of clubs. The wine bar we were in now was a far cry from the house-party swinger's do I had been to; the bar didn't look as if it had beds, for a start. One of the girls in the agency had mentioned a posh swinger's club she knew of where you were vetted before you joined and were only allowed in if you looked right, and another girl mentioned one that was only for eighteen- to thirty-five-year-olds. Going by the older couple we had followed in, it definitely wasn't going to be one of those.

Although Mr Swing was a member, he didn't know much more than I did – or even that much. I could hear music as I descended the steps into the basement bar, Mr Swing behind me. It didn't sound clubby. I was a bit apprehensive. At least when I went to the fetish club I had known I could leave any time I wanted to; here, on my client's arm, I was a lady of the night, his partner, and would have to stay. We had worked out our stories beforehand: he worked in the City and I did something in the art world.

We signed in, paying some sort of fee to the host couple. The hostess marked a card and put it back in an index box on the desk, and both of them smiled as we handed over our coats and they welcomed us in. Mr Host took us over to the bar, showing us around as he went, all the time looking down my front. The too-small net bra gave me ample cleavage.

'Over there is the snug. It's quieter, just for chatting,' he said, pointing to the corner on our right. There were a few couples there already, sitting on the sofas.

'Over there, behind the black curtain, is the dance floor, and that's where the naughtiness commences.' He winked at me as we approached the bar. My gent was looking around eagerly. I was paying more attention to our enigmatic host – after all, he was running the show, and if anyone was going to smell a rat in his camp then it would be him. I smiled, sweetly content that he wouldn't suss I was a hooker: there were certainly women dressed more sluttily than I was in the room.

The host couple must have been in their mid-forties, and he was very grey, with a shiny bald spot on top which the overhead spotlights bounced off. The hostess, who had slicked-back brown hair and the red lace of her lingerie poking through the deep-cut V of her smart tie dress, was obviously a submissive sort, as she looked up at her husband all the time – not in an obvious way, but you could tell who wore the trousers in that relationship. I was very interested at that point, seeing all the content couples around, how they could have sex with others and not feel jealous and fight about it. In my experience, jealousy was the killer in a relationship. I had been with many men who were scared to death of their wives finding out they had been with other women. They said that their wives would leave them, throw them out or divorce them if they found out they were seeking the comfort their wife was no longer providing elsewhere. For them, seeing an escort was less messy and easier than having an affair. I was very sceptical about what really went on with swingers. From the little I had heard from my clients, it tended to be the last stab at a failing relationship, a means to get the wife more involved and spice up a stagnant marriage.

Mr Host left us at the bar, saying, 'Enjoy,' over his shoulder, and went to attend to another couple who had just come in. I smiled, looking at the curtain over the supposed dance floor, which ran from one wall to the other, and from the ceiling to the floor, and turned to my companion for the night. He was looking at a couple sitting across the room on one of the sofas who were chatting away to each other.

'So, do you like her?' I whispered in his ear, as he tried to get the attention of the barman.

'Her over there? No, not really my thing. Do you?'

I looked over at the couple again. The man had a moustache and definitely a paunch hidden under his smart jacket, but he was OK, looked friendly enough, and she was a curvy blonde.

'She's cute, but he's not really my type either.' I had decided that, as he was paying me, I might as well say I liked the couples he liked. It wasn't as if I was fussy about looks really, especially when I was on the clock.

I caught the barman's eye as I leaned over the bar. I had found that cleavage was a fabulous invention for catching a barman's eye. Hell, any man's eye!

I was wondering what was behind the curtain. No one had come out or gone in yet, despite the few couples who had arrived after we had. As we were there on the dot, I had the feeling it was a bit too soon for anything to be kicking off, let alone the naughtiness implied by our host. Mr Swing ordered our drinks and we took a seat on one of the sofas on the far wall.

'Looks like we are here a little early,' he murmured, reading my mind.

'So, what goes on behind the curtain? You've been here before, right?' I asked, sipping my fizzy drink, and motioning over to the area on the other side of the room as another couple walked in.

'Er, no, I haven't been here before, they hold events in lots of different clubs and bars. The curtain is to stop the bar staff getting embarrassed at the dirty dancing that happens on the dance floor . . . Supposedly.'

'Supposedly there's dirty dancing, or supposedly it's there to protect the staff from seeing the couples actually having sex behind it?'

He shrugged. 'There are other clubs outside London which are specially kitted out as sex clubs for swingers. The events aren't held in bars or normal clubs like they are here in the city – or so I hear.' He rambled on about things he had heard as I people-watched and nodded.

Our host was still talking to the couple he had gone to greet. The woman had just taken off her coat, handing it to her casually attired hubby by her side. She was topless, wearing only strained fishnet stockings. Flesh bulged out over her suspenders and big knickers. The flustered host hurriedly said a few words, out of our range of hearing, a strained smile on his face. The hubby put his wife's coat over her shoulders and they headed for the black curtain, chatting animatedly and giggling. After a couple of seconds the hubby came back out and went out to the entrance to hang up his wife's coat.

'That told her,' Mr Swing grunted beside me. 'I'm not sure what happens behind the curtain really, I've never been back there. The lady who came with me before didn't want to, so we didn't. Do you want to?'

I nodded slowly, and that perked him up. He was obviously as intrigued as I was, and he was on the point of leaving the sofa when I put my hand on his knee and said that maybe we should wait for a few more people to arrive so that there was actually something to check out when we did go. He nodded, and we chatted about the other couples in the room. Some of them were looking at us, too. I got a wink from an older lady with a toyboy on her arm. Mr Swing didn't like that at all. He was too young for me anyhow. I smiled to the older woman. She was friendly enough but, I gauged, definitely not at all my companion's type.

The basement room was starting to fill up, to the point where I couldn't see who was going into the curtained-off room. There were couples of all different ages. Most were what I expected, but there were a few attractive couples in their twenties, who were drawing the attention of my thirty-four-year-old companion. We eventually left the comfort of our perving position on the sofa and started to mingle. It was all very civilized – names were exchanged, jobs and interests discussed; the normal sort of dinner-party conversation really. Only one older couple mentioned going behind the curtain, inviting us. They went off, Mr Swing saying we would join them later, but I had the feeling not that he wasn't keen on going behind the curtain but that he wasn't keen on them. He was starting to drool over a pretty, shy brunette on the arm of a rather tall, older gent. Of the two, he was doing all the talking. My gent whispered in my ear. 'She's nice – should we go and talk to them?' He obviously hadn't even noticed the older gent she was with. He looked more like her father than her partner.

'OK,' I said. I smiled at her and started to totter over to them to make our introductions, only to be intercepted by the hostess taking hold of my arm. 'How are you doing? Enjoying yourselves?' she said. She giggled a bit, smiling at Mr Swing and grabbing his arm too. By the time I had managed to pass her off to another couple, the tall man and the brunette had vanished, which meant one of two things: either they had left or, more likely, they were behind the curtain. Before Mr Swing had a chance to state the obvious, I was hooking an arm in his and teetering towards a flap in the curtain. I pushed my way keenly through into the darker, much louder room behind.

It took a few moments to make out what the shapes were in the near dark, but my eyes quickly adjusted. Some couples were slow dirty-dancing in the room and others, in various states of undress, were perched on the few chairs that were dotted around the walls. We took a turn around the floor and caught sight of the naked, fish-netted wife in one corner, her hubby seated beside her. He was talking to another lady, his arm over her shoulder and his hand down her blouse, fumbling in her bra. His wife looked totally unconcerned. It was only as we got closer that we made out a head in her lap. A man on his knees was bobbing up and down between her legs, and the look on her face was actually one of content rather than unconcern.

The dancefloor was fairly crowded, but I could just make out the tall man dancing with his lady. I caught a glimpse of another couple, too, just as the lady touched the arm of another passing couple. The gesture was reciprocated and the four moved off to some vacant chairs to chat. It wasn't hard to keep my dance partner in a position where I could watch what would happen next. I'd quickly clicked that the brief touch was a signal: if someone touched you it meant they liked you, and if you liked them too, you touched them back, basically indicating that you would like to play with them. If you didn't touch back, just shaking your head and smiling, it meant you were not really interested: thanks but no thanks. It also looked as if the ladies were the ones with the power. More often than not it was the woman who approached another woman. I had noticed the odd one or two single men, but either they were there alone or their partners hadn't come into the draped-off area or they were in the loos. In any case the single men had less luck, if any at all, in approaches.

I gained back some of my dancing partner's atten-tion by slowly rubbing my chest up against his. He was watching two couples still on the dancefloor but dancing on the spot. The women were facing each other and kissing. One of them was stripped to the waist and the man from the other couple was handling her boobs. The other man had his hands up the other woman's skirt. I leaned in to Mr Swing and slid my hand down his back, leaving my hand on his bum and steering him towards the tall man, who I could still make out on the other side of the room. We made better progress once my partner had the cute brunette in his sights and realized what I was up to.

The tall man smiled at me as we drew near. They were chatting to a nearby couple as they danced, but it was easy to approach as they drew aside to make room for us. I touched the brunette's arm and introduced us both. There was only a slight hesitation while she looked up at the tall man, and at his nod she put her arm around my waist and I broke away from Mr Swing so that she could lean in close to introduce themselves too. The couple they had been talking to were in their mid-thirties and fairly attractive. They also sidled up and, before I knew it, there were hands everywhere, which gained a brooding look from Mr Swing, still keeping his eye on the brunette. He stroked a hand down her back and she didn't mind in the least.

I was now standing with my back to the tall man. The other woman, a curvy blonde, had managed to untie my dress. The front slid open and long fingers snuck up from behind me to rub my nipples over the low-cut net bra as the blonde leaned in to kiss me. I got a mouthful of tongue as the fingers tweaked my nipples. Out of the corner of my eye I could see that the brunette was getting much the same nipple treatment from Mr Swing. The blonde's partner's hands were around her, and now they were stroking along my sides. I moved down from the kiss to find one of her nipples to suck. I saw a dark grin from Mr Swing. He stopped the brunette from unbuttoning his shirt and turned her towards me.

I had raised my head from the blonde, who was now moaning gustily while someone fingered her, and now both my nipples were being sucked, one by each woman. Hands supported me from behind, and there was a firm erection nuzzling into me as I leaned back. The blonde moved up to kiss me again and the tall man behind me pushed the brunette's head down my body. I felt small hands push my knickers down my legs, and her mouth latched on to my wet lips, now directly in front of her, licking me while her partner's hand pushed her head into me. I fumbled with the erection behind me but he removed my hands and placed them on the head in my crotch.

The blonde had by now made it back down to my nipples. I glanced over to the near wall, where Mr Swing had pulled up a seat and had his hand down his trousers. He looked quite content, watching the goings on, and I slowly moved around so he had a slightly better view of the people pleasuring me and what they were up to. It seemed that hands from everywhere were holding me, nearly lifting me off my feet. The brunette buried her head as I climaxed on her face, loud enough that it drew a tight crowd. The brunette looked pleased as Punch, and the tall man bent to kiss her wet face, escorting her out of the room as she waved to me. I had repositioned myself in front of the blonde, as her husband fingered her roughly. She had his cock in her hand, wanking away. I was aiming to leave them when Mr Swing sidled up and handed me a condom, gesturing to the blonde's partner's cock, then re-took his seat to watch the three of us.

They were more than happy for me to rubber him up and start to suck him. We moved back towards the chairs, and I sat down next to Mr Swing, still with a mouthful of cock, while the blonde's partner continued to finger her, jabbing away, all three of us in a strange sexual daisy chain of motion. My voyeur sat back in his chair and looked on as I sunk my nails in the balls of the cock I was sucking and gently squeezed. With a shudder it came in a hot rush as the balls exploded into the mint-flavoured rubber. The blonde sucked him clean and, after giving us a goodbye wink, they both headed for the loos on the other side of the curtain.

We had been on the dancefloor longer than I realized, and Mr Swing, his trousers looking more than a snug fit, was ready to leave. He'd seen more than enough, he said, to keep him in lustful thoughts for quite some time and he was especially impatient to get back to the car for a blow job. A moment was all it took for us to slip out, retrieve our coats and find the car in order to grant his wish.

Mr Panic: Part 2

He swore loudly and ran from the room in a flap, leaving me bent over the uncomfortable arm of a chair, the very

248

painful position he had put me in. I hadn't had the chance to turn over before he left the room, so I didn't realize why he had. One minute he was bad-shagging away, pushing in, then pulling all the way out, then slamming back in, without a clue where he was aiming, and the next he was gone. I eased myself up, feeling a bit numb and sore, and noticed the blood on my leg. Damn, the man had been too rough again; he had very nearly caused damage last time because of it. It all made sense now: he had seen blood and fled to the bathroom. With him being so paranoid about his health, I could just imagine how panicked he would be at the sight of it. I was more in need of the bathroom than he was, but I could already hear the shower on full blast. I could just bet he was scrubbing himself down. I fished my wet wipes from my bag and tidied myself up.

It was a good ten minutes before he came out, looking ashen-faced. I sat fully dressed on the bed, waiting. I needed more than a deep breath to calm myself as he started to go on and on about how I shouldn't be working if I was on my period; the agency shouldn't let me, bla bla bla. I tried to say that I wasn't due on for ages, and that he had torn me, but he wasn't listening. His mind was ticking over too fast, speculating whether he would have caught Aids or not. Here we go. Any minute now, despite the fact that he was wearing a rubber and, as he himself had said, he hadn't had any blood on him, he was going to demand my clinic results to make sure. If I was unlucky, he would call the agency to complain – not that the Lush would give two hoots: it wasn't as if he was a regular client of hers; he had only come to her because he had found me after I moved from my previous agency. I resigned myself to the fact that I would have to go to my clinic and get them to write a letter or print out a certificate of my last test, a month back, to keep him happy, as he was really working himself up into a state, saying it was God punishing him for some reason or some such religious rubbish. It wasn't going to be good enough, he reckoned, to hear from my clinic. *What?*

I was getting a headache and, not only that, I was starting to sting, and all because he was a lousy lay. And now he wanted me to drag myself out of bed the next morning to go with him to a private sex clinic that could give us blood tests and get the results back to us that day. He would pay for the tests, he said. I took it he wasn't going to pay for my time that night. He was starting to say that I shouldn't really work until I was better, meaning until my 'period' was over, and that if I didn't show up the next morning, he really should, out of duty, phone up the agency and make a fuss; I might be giving other people nasty things too. It sounded suspiciously like a back-handed form of blackmail to me, but I didn't want him calling the Lush and telling her I might be contagious; I didn't want it to go that far.

To my mind, he was being totally illogical. There was nothing wrong with me. I always played safe, even on my occasional weekends with Mr Tux. I hadn't had any accidents and all my tests were coming back clear. I was certainly healthier than the chainsmoking doctor I saw at the clinic. In any case, given the state Mr Panic was in, and if he was intent on making a fuss, it could be very damaging to my reputation. It didn't matter that he was wrong; just the whiff of there being something up could be catastrophic. If it got around the agency and another girl talked, no client would come near me, and even if I went to another agency, with the way girls moved between them, it wouldn't take long for the misinformation to travel. I wasn't happy about it but it had to be done.

I should have felt smug the next morning at the clinic, as he still looked preoccupied, as if he hadn't slept. I tried to feel sympathy for him, but it was difficult. He went in first and, after waiting in a small room for what seemed like an age, it was my turn. The male doctor sympathized with me when I said that Mr Panic had been wrong that I was on my period. Mr Panic had blamed it all on me, passing me off as a new girlfriend.

The doctor proceeded to give me a full exam, rather than just taking blood, which, I gathered, had been Mr Panic's idea. The doctor commented on the small tear he found. I told him what had happened and he was definitely on my side. The only advantage for me in being there and having a full check-up was my peace of mind. I was now sure the damage that had been done had already healed fairly well and, as I had thought, that it wasn't worse.

The doctor was a friendly chap and, after he had finished taking my blood and swabs, he went out into the waiting room as I got dressed to find Mr Panic, to have a 'word', he said, much to my amusement. I could hear the doctor giving Mr Panic a faint dressing-down in the other room, which cheered me up no end, then I joined a sheepish Mr Panic, who bustled us out, saying he would rather phone in for the results that afternoon than wait. He charitably said that he would let me know the result later – the cheek! At that he left me to find my car, heading off in the opposite direction. I wasn't too worried, and I was right not to be, as he called that evening. I was 'lucky', he said; he was clear and so was I.

He was ecstatic about the negative result and even suggested that, now he knew I was 'clean' and because he had my mobile number (I had given it to him so he could call me to arrange meeting up at the clinic), he would be able to call me without going through the agency. He said he didn't like going in there, and now he wouldn't need to again; I would have the dubious honour of seeing him privately. Oh joy!

I had phoned in sick to get off work the night before and taken two days off. I always had to take a few days off when I had tests, as the needle left a mark on my arm. I didn't want to go to work looking like a junkie. I was less than happy about losing a couple of days' work and I was tempted to tell him where to stuff his suggestion. I chickened out in the end. I just didn't want the hassle. I said I couldn't that night but would call him the next day. He rang off, full of the joys of spring, 'happy to still be alive'. Straight away I made a new category on my phone; he was the first on my barred list. I swore never to darken his dick again.

Avalon was a tall bi Australian girl with beautiful eyes and a pretty face. She was curvy, long-legged and big-busted, but by no means looked like any of the other girls. OK, she was really tall – six foot three at least – but for some reason she had shaved her head. She was completely bald and liked being that way. With her long eyelashes and doe eyes, it actually looked good on her. She was the most unusual-looking girl I had ever seen working for an agency.

When she first turned up, Ms Lush was very keen on getting her to wear a wig, as she said no one would pick her if she didn't, but Avalon piped up that she had been earning elsewhere and had had no difficulties with being chosen and, if no one picked her, she would be the one who was losing out, so what was the problem? Ms Lush, having lost three girls to another agency the week before, was obviously keen to make up the numbers, so she said she would give Avalon and her friend a go. We were all mystified as to how the Lush had come to employ Avalon, but a little digging around and a long discussion with her friend Daphne, who was American, had her spilling that Avalon was quite submissive; she liked a bit of pain and so did the 'pornstar experience'. Daphne whispered and winked. 'You know – she likes it up the bum and does everything, hard core.' No wonder the Lush had taken her on then; she didn't have many girls who would do that sort of thing.

The tall Aussie didn't look at all submissive though –

far from it: she was quite dominant-looking, with her hard stare and robust stature. I wasn't into women as such, but if I were, I would fancy Avalon: she was beautiful. No, sod that, she was stunning, hair or no hair – and that begged the question: was she shaved all over? My mind had wandered during the conversation I was having with Daphne. She was explaining that they were on a round-the-world trip, making money any way they could. She'd pretty much come along for the ride.

She was a short, small-busted brunette, so she didn't have much going for her in the escort phone-request department, and she said herself that, with her gymnastic skills, she earned better working with a stationary pole than 'a floppy one'. She didn't really need to say that she wasn't too much into men. Now, women, on the other hand . . . Avalon was not so much into making money but was out and out up for experiencing anything she could along the way, the more off the wall the better. Daphne was the saner of the two and, although slight, with nondescript dark, straight hair, she was very pretty in her own right; it was just that she was overshadowed by her friend.

It was a surprise to all of us when Avalon bounded up the stairs and nabbed the first client of the day, much to the bemusement of the Lush. According to her, the longstanding client, who usually booked shorter orientals, had said that he had chosen her for her novelty value, as she was so unusual looking, rather than out of lust. Unlike Layla, with her ample charms, me with my girl-next-door looks or Anita with her Nordic beauty, Avalon was picked from curiosity; it seemed she was larger than life. I guess the fact that she would take it in every hole helped too. I was intrigued: did being so big make it easier for her? She said she liked being submissive, she liked being degraded by men, but somehow I couldn't see how anyone could degrade her – there was far too much to her, in terms of both stature and personality. I could just see her in my mind's eye shagging Daphne senseless with a big strap-on. Now there was a thought. But what was I doing? I was drifting off and thinking far too deeply about a girl I had hardly met or got to know. Maybe I was more into girls than I thought, after all.

Daphne had met Avalon while working in a Vegas stripclub. I asked her if her friend was always hyper, and Daphne said yes, she was like that naturally, as far as she could tell from having travelled with her for a year; it wasn't drugs, if that was what I was hinting at. Daphne wasn't exactly a wallflower herself and, with all the yoga positions she did in the lounge while waiting for the buzzer, she put all of us lazy sofa lizards to shame.

Both of them were settling in well. One day, Avalon made her very kinky hello in the shortest skirt possible and talked the client into a two-girl booking. Daphne had just been sent off to a booking in a Park Lane hotel, and I was surprised to find Avalon dragging me along with her. She was such a force of nature, I had no way of saying no, even if I had wanted to, so gathering our coats and bags, we headed off to the client's apartment, which was three streets away in a smart apartment block.

Now, from what I could gather, the client Mr Lesbian Lover was into watching Avalon and me make out while he wanked; he would join in later. She had told me all this in a rush as we had got ready to leave the agency. It was fine by me. I had done girl-on-girl before – not normally with girls I hadn't known, granted – but I was by now itching to see her naked and I couldn't see the harm. After all, you can't turn into a lesbian overnight, just by looking at a naked lady – can you? Avalon had the bemused client strip her. He took a seat on a chair by the bed. He was goggle-eyed as she unzipped his fly and started to wank him. Then it all kicked off. Despite being so much taller than me, when she was on her knees, the tables were turned from the get-go, as she had taken out of her bag and presented me with the longest dildo I had ever seen. Now, I have seen some long rubber phalluses before, but this thing was a snake, and she was all but waving it at me to use on her. She bent over the client so he could watch me, now in my lingerie, put my hands to her hips and raise her from her kneeling position. She now had a faceful of cock, and I slowly eased her cheeks apart and gently slid in the rubber head of the dildo as she wiggled back on to it.

The erection she was sucking lustily must have almost choked her as the client thrust up to get a better look, shunting her backwards. That rammed the dildo in as far as it would go but, even so, there was a great deal of length left – more than enough for me to play with and slide up too. In a jumble of legs and arms, we were all on the bed, Avalon underneath and somehow the client still pumping away in her mouth. She squeezed his balls to make him shudder, and I pulled the dildo slowly in and out, trying to get out of my underwear and the client out of the rest of his clothes. So much for him watching and then joining in; we were in danger of him popping too soon, at this rate, which would not have been good.

Wrangling the client out of his trousers, I took charge, making him slow down a pace or two. I ordered Avalon to stay on the bed, then knelt so that I was poised over her head. I looked down at her to keep her there. Her cheeky grin was not just for show. She looked up at my now uncovered pussy and the client eagerly looked on, too. I was hoping she would understand that we had to drag the show out for longer than she had been. Almost before I caught the glint in her eye, and to the very appreciative moan of the client, she stuck her tongue out and pulled my hips down to sit on her face, skewering me on her waggling tongue and sucking with her hot mouth.

It was a bit of a shock, as she was the first girl to really go down on me properly. Most working girls normally fake it; I knew all the girls I worked with did. Girls said they were bi, but it was all for show, an extra selling point. It didn't matter if you actually were or not. You might have a girl's head in your crotch from time to time while guys looked on during duos, but no girl actually wet, open-mouth kissed down there, let alone sucked or tongued you. If you could act well, you just didn't need to go that far.

This was different. My shocked intake of breath came from enjoyment, and she set to work, tonguing my clit. She was gorgeous below me, all soft skin and smelling of vanilla. I completely forgot the client was there, wanking away and willing us on. I didn't know what to do with myself; should I reciprocate? Now the client was on his knees and between hers, licking her out as she was me, beating me to it. I was feeling a bit light-headed, which wasn't good at that point; the girl had a mouth like a vacuum cleaner and wouldn't let go.

I ooohed and ahhhhed, and the client was more than happy, playing with my nipples, as I stroked hers below me. Avalon stopped for a moment but only because he wanted her bent over so he could ride her doggie-style. They got into position, but she took me with her, flipping me over easily, as she was nearly twice my weight, and she continued lapping away after we had rubbered him up. He rode her and then me, as she lay next to us, playing with the dildo for us to watch.

The client pounded away in me until he noticed that she had bent the double dildo in two and was now buggering herself with the other end as well. His eyes nearly popping out of their sockets, he wanted to swap again, and he slid up her arse, with her on her back beneath him, and before he had made two strokes he came over her in a shuddering heap. I just sat there and watched, trying to get my breath back. Now that had been amazing: she had just swallowed his cock up to the hilt all the way up her bumhole, and it wasn't as if he was badly endowed either. Amazing, and I was truly in lust with her tongue – it was just the same as when Tony used to lick me out when I sat on his face, but Avalon was all soft curves to his hard muscle. I shivered at the thoughts that kept popping up in my head of her beneath me and me ordering her to do what I willed, then started to get off the bed to clean up, letting her and Mr Lesbian Lover, who looked a lot worse for wear, lie on the bed resting.

The guy lay still, panting, and I had to tug her and make eye signals towards the bathroom before she noticed that time was nearly up. If I hadn't pulled her away, I'm sure she would have pounced on either him or I for seconds – and there was I thinking that *I* had a sexual appetite. I had finally met my match in Avalon, but it wasn't helping us get dressed and back to the agency on time. The client was looking happy. I didn't really notice or remember anything else about him. He was an average type of guy, nothing in particular to note, and I had been more intent on my buxom playmate than on paying much attention to him. He was just another face. She, on the other hand – well, the minx was something else. If she had been a guy, it would have been easy but she had Daphne with her, and I didn't want to step on anyone's toes. Not that I wanted a girlfriend to add to my list of people to call in case of horny emergencies. Or did I? Hmmm, sometimes too much thinking is not a good thing.

I was only going to get into trouble if I wasn't careful. Avalon might have been acting, for all I knew. I was pondering all this on the way back to the agency, trying to keep up with her long strides, as she ambled along chattering away about where she and Daphne were going to go that night. She had just called and, as it was past 9 p.m. and Avalon didn't have to go back to work, they were going to meet up back at the agency and go off clubbing. I was going to see if I could get another client that night.

I liked Daphne; we got on really well. She would natter about working in some stripclub in the US and I would tell her what little I knew about the British ones, as she was interested in going back to stripping; escorting wasn't really for her. She said that she missed dancing but was thinking of going back later in the year when they made it to Oz, if they 'got that far'. She motioned over to her tall sidekick, who was chatting to the Russians, trying to squeeze details of late-night clubs and other places they could go to after work out of them.

I wouldn't want to cross Daphne. She was nice, and I had the impression she liked Avalon more than she let on. You only had to watch her face light up when they were in the same room together to feel how possessive she was of her. Avalon was totally oblivious, caught up in her own world and living a self-centred life of abandon and lust. No one around her really mattered, which was her only fault, as far as I could tell.

'I think I'm a lesbian,' I half joked to Layla after awaking from a torrid dream the next day. It had featured me with a strap-on and a naked, bound Avalon bent over a white-leather whipping bench before me.

'Ha! You? You are NO lesbian.' She said it deadpan, although I could tell she was slightly amused.

'I could be.' I was a bit miffed.

'You are no more a muff-diver than I am, you like your men too much. Don't forget: I've been in a room when you shag them senseless,' she snorted.

She had a point. 'You don't have to be a rug-muncher to be a lesbian, do you? Can you be a munchee? Is there such a word?' I quizzed. I wasn't really looking for an answer. 'Ever thought I could be bi?' Layla chortled even more when I suggested that.

'Ha, titty, ha. I don't think being paid to do it counts, babe.' She was very amused now.

'Why? Wouldn't you love me any more if I turned a little lesbian?' I put on a sulking voice, just for the fun of it.

'Babe, if you turn a little lesbian, for free, let me know her name, and then I will believe you.' She all but smirked.

I tittered and let her bend my ear, talking about her plans.

In the end, I didn't have a chance to get into trouble, as I was busy and it was only a matter of weeks before Avalon and Daphne moved on. They promised to send a postcard from Paris, but we never did get one, if one was ever sent. Like many other girls I had worked with in the past, they just disappeared.

Afterword: Not the End

'So who's with me?' Tandy was waiting by the foot of the lounge steps ready to leave the agency after a particularly slow night.

'Harvey Nicks, fifth floor?' queried Sonya. She and a few of the other girls had been nattering about going to posh hotel bars and hanging around to see if they could pick up any clients. It hadn't just been a slow night but a slow week. It had been getting progressively worse at the agency, with fewer and fewer men coming in. We hadn't really taken much notice at first, and when regular girls from other agencies came in for interviews to work at ours, they said that ours was busier than theirs. The influx of new girls was worrying, though, because when loyal girls from one agency start looking for new agencies to work at, thinking things must be better elsewhere, it's a sign that something is up.

Some of the girls were getting desperate and had decided that, if the clients weren't coming into the agency, they would go and find them themselves. The only person who wasn't worried in the slightest was Layla. She had all but moved in with her musician boyfriend and had been working less and less, until she was only working week-ends, just in case her new man found out what she was up to. She had told him what she had done in the past but didn't feel the need to tell him she was working as an escort now, and she had even found herself a normal job working in a posh shop during the week as cover. Now, on the verge of moving in with him, she was thinking of quitting altogether and moving the last box of stuff she had at mine to his. His flatmate had moved out weeks before, so there was nothing stopping her. He was a very nice guy and they got on really well. I was happy for her.

Layla eventually quit one weekend when there were lots of girls on shift and no clients came in. I wasn't surprised. I was still doing well, as I had amassed quite a few regular clients by that point, and they still called for me, so I was busy even though, all around me, girls were getting a bit desperate. We couldn't figure out what was going on. Even Ms Lush was confounded: it wasn't just happening at her sit-in agency; it seemed that men had just stopped going to any agency. Things had been slowing down for a few months, and a couple of agencies had shut, but the long-standing, popular ones like ours had still been doing OK – enough to cover the bills at any rate. There were always slow times, such as just after New Year, and busy times, such as Christmas, and summer, when all the girls out and about in shorter skirts got men's blood up and they came in looking for some fun. We just took this for one of these times, thinking that maybe it was the financial market, which had been rocked, causing a ripple effect. Tandy said she had heard the same thing had happened in the eighties. Girls had been able to charge a fortune, as there were fewer of them, but then the financial market had crashed or some-thing, and fewer men were out spending. The girls, who had been able to live on Park Lane and had shoe-boxes of cash under their beds, they had been so busy, virtually overnight had to sell their cars and move out, dropping their rates to get any work at all. Tandy said that it would pass; men don't stop being horny just because of financial restraint. Things would pick up.

I had been settled at Ms Lush's agency for over a year by then, and had made some good friends and had some good clients as regs. The agency had been going for ten years, so it was a bit of a surprise when Ms Lush told me in confidence when I came in for an early shift that she was going to close it in two weeks' time. The lease was due to run out and the landlord of the property was doubling her rent. As he thought the sit-in agency was really some sort of brothel and that it was raking it in, he wanted £100,000 a year rent, which was just silly. As Ms Lush said, the agency hardly made two-thirds of that amount as it was. I didn't know if I believed her or not, but she said there was no point in starting up elsewhere. She had had enough of working late nights after so many years and was going to move to live near her daughter; running an agency was bad for her health. I suppose it wasn't surprising really, but I was betting that, rather than the late nights, it was more likely the bottle she drank dry every night and the amount she smoked that was bad for her health.

'Don't tell any of the other girls,' she said, 'they don't deserve to know. I'm only telling you because you're the only one that has been loyal to me, and I appreciate it and know you can keep your mouth shut.' I understood what she was saying. Reading between the lines, she was telling me it was OK to give out my number to my regular clients or to keep their numbers, so that when the agency closed they could find me and I would still have work.

'Why don't you tell the others?' I didn't like to think of her suddenly springing it on the girls and them being made unemployed overnight.

'Them? They'll live. If I tell them now, most will go off to work for other agencies, and then I'll have no girls to work for the next two weeks, despite the fact that they have to work two weeks before they get their deposit back. They won't care. I need the money that will come in as there's no way I'm going to get my deposit back for renting here.' She lit up a fag and took a drag.

I only gave my favourite regulars my number in the end, thinking that I didn't want to be bothered with the gents who got on my nerves. That would keep me afloat for a while, until I found another way of picking up clients. It wasn't as if I was going to risk the bars and have to barter with men, I knew I wasn't very good at that anyhow, and the agencies that were still open were in just as bad a state as ours and, after ours closed, they would be flooded with girls; they could take their pick. There was always the option of putting an advert in the paper where the agencies advertised. A few girls did, but I wasn't sure if I wanted to deal with the idiots who might phone up to mess me around. In the past, Tandy had mentioned that if she left the agency she might consider running girls so, if I was desperate, I could always give her a call if I needed to keep my hand in and gain new clients but, for the moment, sticking with the regular clients, ones that had my number and I already knew were safe from seeing them from the agency, was a better bet.

I'd be a sort of independent escort. That would be novel. I hadn't had to deal with clients on the phone before, I had always been sent or there had been a receptionist to deal with them, but in its favour there was the fact that I wouldn't have to give a cut to someone else. Most of my regs, as they called for me to be sent to them and didn't come into the office, hadn't had to pay the agency fee separately, so they didn't know that the agency's cut was around 30 per cent. As far as they knew, all the money they gave me came to me so, being independent, I could pocket the agency fee too and keep all of it, no questions asked. I could also take my time if I wanted to and not have to rush off. I could dress how I liked and even go back to being a redhead. Most of all, I wouldn't have to sit around and wait to be told where to go; I could make my own plans.

The thought of being independent, free to sit at home all day or to do other things until my phone rang, calling me into action, and not having to hang around in a lounge full of bitchy girls and cigarette smoke was an enticing one, at least until I worked out what to do next. I could do with a holiday, too. I had got into the rut of working solidly, nearly every day now. My play companions had pretty much run their course. Tony was still away, and I had had to call an end to my relationship with Mr Tux, too, as I had noticed I was beginning to become far too attached for my own liking. I didn't want him to leave his wife for me and I definitely didn't want to mess my life up and complicate it with a full-blown relationship; there was far too much yet to discover in the world.

Who knew? Maybe I could change my frame of mind, from working for an agency to working for myself. I could go off on holiday with Mr Professor, one of my favourite regular Mr Average clients, for example. He'd pay for an exotic holiday, the tickets and meals – not for my time, but that would be OK. The other girls all said disdainfully that it was like giving a client a freebie, but if it was a holiday I wanted to go on …? He was a nice, older chap, and we got along really well. What was to stop me flitting off to the Seychelles with him in a few weeks' time, as he had asked? With an indefinite amount of time off pending, I found myself at a crossroads.

What *was* a working girl turned escort to do when her agency closed? Join another sit-in agency, try one of those new online escort agencies the girls had been talking about or – gulp – take the plunge without the safety net of an agency and fly solo?

Well, how hard can it be to go all the way and be totally independent?

Handy Hints for Hookers

Every escort has a shag bag – her work bag – full of the things she can't do without. What she puts in it depends on the working girl. With everything I take with me, my shag bag is not exactly a small evening clutch but that doesn't mean I take a carpet bag with me either. I use a smart, plain shoulder bag, preferably one with a compartment on the outside, which is useful for holding condoms and makes it quick and easy to find them. I personally have two work bags, the second an exact double also containing everything on my list. I keep them both by the door ready to go, so I don't have to tip out the contents of one to empty it into the other. One bag is black and the other is cream, so they go with everything. (Yes, I really am like this and, no, I was never a Girl Guide.)

If the bag doesn't have lots of pockets inside, I use small clear zip-lock make-up bags to hold things so that they are easy to find and don't get lost at the bottom of the bag. There's nothing worse than having a horny gent champing at the bit and having to tip out everything just to find a butt plug.

My Shag Bag Supplies

*My top-five must-haves

• *At least ten condoms of at least three sizes. (Also needed to cover toys to keep them clean in my bag). Ten, even if I have only one client and he only gets to do it once. I don't give them the chance of using the tired old excuse of 'accidentally' taking a rubber off/it coming off and then wanting you and pushing you to do something without one to finish. (This is mainly tried on new, green girls, who may only take one or two condoms with them to a booking.)

• *Lube. No matter who you are, the wetter you are the better. (Tip: Also good as a dab below the eye for refreshing dry make-up quickly.)

• *Work phone, for agency to call me on and a number to give other girls. Have a cheap phone just for work; there are just too many reasons not to use a personal phone. Have a spare, charged phone battery too. (It is Sod's law that you will run out of juice just when you need it.)

• *£20+ for cab fare. Just in case the client doesn't pay. You don't want to be stranded in the middle of nowhere, in the dark, walking a long distance in high heels.

• *Agency card for client. If you lose your phone or reception, you will still have your agency's number to hand. (Also write your agency phone number and that of your safety buddy in your work shoes, in case your bag is snatched.)

- Pocket A–Z, or map of the area you are working in.

- Small vibe toy. Turn the battery around so it doesn't go off by accident.

- Sewing kit. Have different threads and a safety pin, as a lost button on a skirt or a broken zip can be embarrassing when you are crossing a hotel lobby.

- Spare stockings/hold-ups. Men's unkempt nails can cause havoc with your hosiery!

- Folding toothbrush and small tube of toothpaste. For an overnight or dinner booking. (Do not use straight after interacting personally with client in case of aggravating any small break in skin.)

- Your own bar of soap or tube of bodywash. Using lots of different hotel soaps can give you a rash, and you never know where a used bar has been.

- Shower cap. So your hair doesn't get wet and you can leave looking the same as when you came in.

- Hair band/folding brush or comb. So you don't walk out of the door looking like you have been shagged in a hedge or on the hotel roof's heli-pad.

- Make-up. After hours of sitting around waiting in a black hole, you really need it to freshen up and, of course, after a booking.

• Wet wipes. For all those stains that pop up from nowhere when you really don't have time to change.

• Wrapped and ready-to-use latex blocking sponge. Just in case it's the wrong time of the month or a client is a bit heavy-handed.

• Small bottle of massage oil. For normal body massage, not hand jobs, as it can perish the rubber.

• Small pot of massage powder. In case the client doesn't like oil. There is always one!

• Snack bar/protein bar. You may never know where you will end up or when you will next eat, and having your stomach rumble in the middle of a booking can be distracting.

• Mouthwash/gum. To get rid of bad tastes and freshen breath before and after a client.

• Clear lipsalve. No lipstick. Even lipgloss can leave incriminating marks.

• Lighter or matches. In case the client smokes, so he doesn't have to waste time hunting for a light – or popping out and coming back with maybe more than a lighter.

• Small umbrella. Because at some point it will bloody well rain.

• Small pen and a notepad. To doodle on when bored out of your mind.

Safety Notes: For Out-calls

Before you get in a car with a client

• Note the number plate and text it to a friend or safety buddy if you need to.

• Check how many people are in the car – look over at the back seat and even in the boot if you are suspicious. Men have been known to hide a friend there.

• Do not go with anyone wearing gloves.

• If all your senses are screaming that something is wrong, don't go with the client, listen to your instincts. No amount of money is worth risking your safety for.

Once in a car with a client or anyone you don't know

• Don't let the driver use the central-locking mechanism.

• Keep the window open in case you need to shout out.

• Don't let the driver park with your door next to a wall so you are trapped in the car.

• If you find yourself in difficulty, try talking your way out of it, e.g., 'My friend/agency is expecting me back in half an hour and if I don't return she/they will report me missing.'

• If you find yourself in difficulty shout 'fire' as well as 'help' to attract as much attention as possible.

Visiting private addresses

• Make sure someone reliable has the address, knows when you are going and when you are due back. Making friends with another working girl and having her as your safety buddy is to the advantage of both of you.

• If you go in a taxi, ask the driver to wait until the door is opened and wave to the taxi driver as you go in, so that the client will realize that someone knows you are there and has seen you going in.

• Ensure that the client doesn't double-lock the front door behind you.

• If you can, for your own peace of mind, look around and make sure there is only one person in the premises before anything starts, or ask your client to give you 'a tour'.

• Have a good look round so that you are aware of the layout of the flat or house and possible exit points. If you need to, use a plausible excuse and ask to be shown the bathroom or kitchen.

• Keep clients in view when they make you a drink and never leave your drink unattended.

• Check under the bed, if it's viable, and pillows for hidden weapons/objects. You can do it discreetly and not alarm the client by dropping something and having to search for it or by plumping the pillows/pulling back the bedspread and quickly slipping your hand under the pillows as you do.

• Keep your mobile phone with you at all times and memorize the address before you go in, just in case you need to call for help.

• Have a second, charged phone battery in case of emergencies.

• Keep your clothes in one place with your bag in case you need to make a quick exit.

Hotel visits

• When you arrive at a hotel door, stand outside and listen for a minute or two before you knock to see if you can hear other voices in the room.

• Look over the client's shoulder before entering a room, just to make sure he hasn't got a friend you're not expecting with him.

• Casually check out the bathroom on the way through the room or suite if you can, opening the door if necessary, just so you know no one is lurking in there who might pop out and surprise you later.

• When you visit hotels, try and have something discreet to wear when you walk through reception, e.g., a long coat and non-metal heels.

• Remember that, if you need to shout for help, there are lots of other people around in hotels.

• Again, keep your clothes in one place with your handbag, and somewhere on a route from the bed to the door, just in case you need to make a quick exit.

• Never leave your bag unattended. Always take your bag and mobile phone with you to the toilet or bathroom.

• Keep clients in view and, if they make you a drink, watch them make it and do not leave it unattended.

Extra tips

• As with all sex work, use your own condoms and put them on the client yourself.

• Condoms with the British kite mark are better than most.

• Don't wear clothes that could be used to harm or choke you, e.g., scarves, thick necklaces, etc.

• In case your mobile work phone is taken, use a code-name or a letter rather than, e.g., 'Mum', for certain entries, so that no one, even girls you work with, can call or text your family out of spite.

• Try not to take valuable items with you, and no photos of family or anything with your address or real ID on, just in case they fall into the wrong hands.

• Don't have your address with your keys in your bag. If you have to have your keys with you, just put your work phone number on them in case they get lost. (Non-work-related: put your phone number in gloves, or your coat collar, or slip a card into your coat pocket so that, if the item gets lost in a check-in cloakroom, an attendant can phone you if they find it.)

• Learn to recognize your own limits with alcohol or drugs. If you are off your face or even mildly drunk your instincts and defences will be muddled. Having your safety compromised isn't very professional.

• Always plan your journey to and from any venue with care. Know where you are going in advance.

• Make sure you have enough money on you for the journey to and back from the booking, just in case it falls through, so you won't be stranded.

• As with all sex work, trust your instincts. If you don't trust your client, for any reason, don't get involved. Many experienced ladies will tell you this is your most useful tool for safety, survival and wellbeing. Personal-attack alarms and other people can only help so far.

• Pick up a copy of the 'Ugly Mugs' or 'dodgy' punters list from your local project or check online warning sites to keep you up to date with what is going on in your area.

• Last but not least, before you leave a house or hotel after a booking, it is best to put your money safe in your bra or inner pocket (not in the top of your stockings as it can slide down and show while you walk). If your bag gets taken from you/you are mugged outside/the client grabs your bag as you leave/hotel security want to check, etc., your hard-earned money will be safe.

SOPHIE MORGAN

THE DIARY OF A SUBMISSIVE

Sophie Morgan is an independent woman in her thirties with a successful journalism career.

Intelligent, witty and sarcastic, she could be the girl next door. Except that Sophie is a submissive; in the bedroom she likes to relinquish her power and personal freedom to a dominant man for their mutual pleasure.

In the wake of Fifty Shades of Grey, here is a memoir that offers the real story of what it means to be a submissive, following Sophie's story as she progresses from her early erotic experiences through to experimenting with her newfound, awakened sexuality. From the endorphin rush of her first spanking right through to punishments the likes of which she couldn't begin to imagine, she explains in frank and explicit fashion the road she travels. But it isn't until she meets James that her boundaries are really pushed. As her relationship with him travels into darker and darker places the question becomes: where will it end? Can she reconcile her sexuality with the rest of her life and is it possible for the perfect man to also be perfectly cruel?

Racy, controversial, but always warm, fun and astoundingly honest this is a fascinating and thought provoking look at a seemingly paradoxical side to human nature and sexuality that no man or woman will be able to put down.

SYLVIA DAY

BARED TO YOU

Our journey began in fire . . .

Gideon Cross came into my life like lightning in the darkness – beautiful and brilliant, jagged and white hot. I was drawn to him as I'd never been to anything or anyone in my life. I craved his touch like a drug, even knowing it would weaken me. I was flawed and damaged, and he opened those cracks in me so easily . . .

Gideon *knew*. He had demons of his own. And we would become the mirrors that reflected each other's most private wounds . . . and desires.

The bonds of his love transformed me, even as I prayed that the torment of our pasts didn't tear us apart . . .

'This is a sophisticated, provocative, titillating, highly erotic, sexually driven read and extremely well done. I enjoyed *Fifty Shades of Grey*, but I loved *Bared to You*' *Swept Away by Romance*

'*Bared to You* has an emotional feel similar to *Fifty Shades of Grey* . . . It is full of emotional angst, scorching love scenes and a compelling storyline' *Dear Author*

'A well written and sexually charged romance with characters who have real depth . . . I would highly recommend *Bared to You*, because it's what *Fifty Shades of Grey* could have been' *The Book Pushers*

'This is an erotic romance that should not be missed. It will make readers fall in love' *Romance Novel News*

He just wanted a decent book to read ...

Not too much to ask, is it? It was in 1935 when Allen Lane, Managing Director of Bodley Head Publishers, stood on a platform at Exeter railway station looking for something good to read on his journey back to London. His choice was limited to popular magazines and poor-quality paperbacks – the same choice faced every day by the vast majority of readers, few of whom could afford hardbacks. Lane's disappointment and subsequent anger at the range of books generally available led him to found a company – and change the world.

'We believed in the existence in this country of a vast reading public for intelligent books at a low price, and staked everything on it'
Sir Allen Lane, 1902–1970, founder of Penguin Books

The quality paperback had arrived – and not just in bookshops. Lane was adamant that his Penguins should appear in chain stores and tobacconists, and should cost no more than a packet of cigarettes.

Reading habits (and cigarette prices) have changed since 1935, but Penguin still believes in publishing the best books for everybody to enjoy. We still believe that good design costs no more than bad design, and we still believe that quality books published passionately and responsibly make the world a better place.

So wherever you see the little bird – whether it's on a piece of prize-winning literary fiction or a celebrity autobiography, political tour de force or historical masterpiece, a serial-killer thriller, reference book, world classic or a piece of pure escapism – you can bet that it represents the very best that the genre has to offer.

Whatever you like to read – trust Penguin.